The New Leader's Playbook

Volume X - 2020

George Bradt's Forbes Articles

Examples of leadership for you to follow.

George Bradt

GHP Press

This is a compilation of the articles I published on Forbes.com in 2020.

In general, I focus on executive onboarding and leading through points of inflection to accelerate transitions, leveraging my own senior line management and consulting experience, as well as my books including "The New Leader's 100-Day Action Plan."

After I'd been contributing to Forbes for two months, I went in to meet the Leadership editor at the time, Fred Allen. He told me that he liked my articles, but bad news would get me more readers. I told him that he had a whole range of contributors, most of which could talk about bad news. I choose to focus on good news and examples of leadership for others to follow.

So, if you're looking for bad news, look elsewhere. The vast majority of articles in The New Leader's Playbook highlight things people do well, leadership worth following and emulating. Read and heed.

George Bradt

How To Win With A Service-Focused Strategy

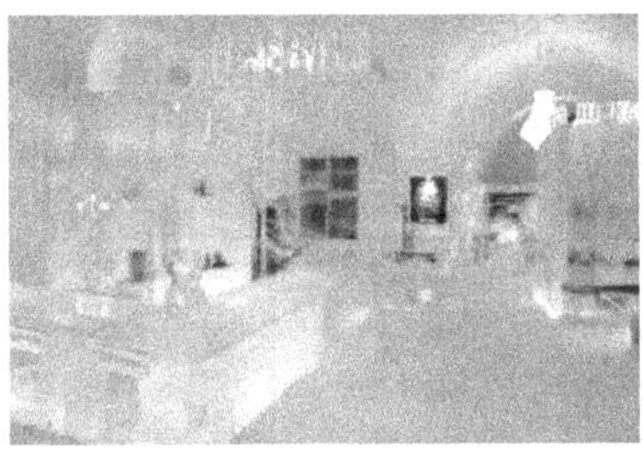

Ice Hotel Luxury Experience LightRocket via Getty Images

As described in my earlier article on What It Takes To Accelerate Through A Strategic Inflection Point, if there is a change in your situation or your ambitions, you need to jump-shift your strategy, organization and operations all together, all at the same time. There are four primary areas of strategic focus: design, produce, deliver, and service. The choice of strategic focus dictates your organizational and operational choices.

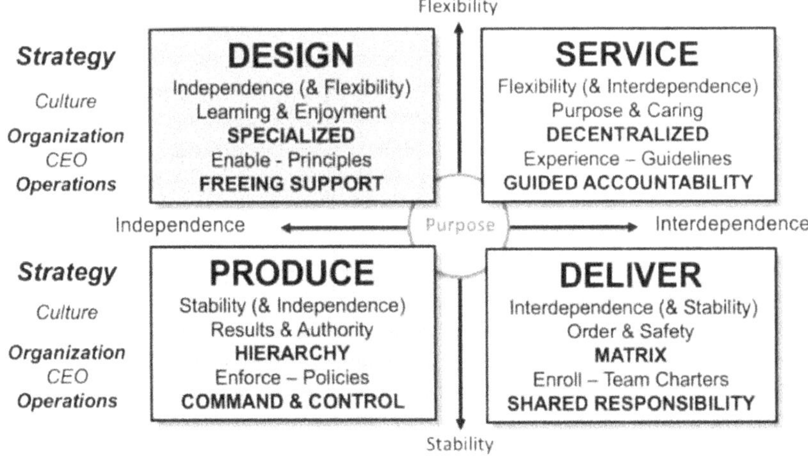

This article is the fourth of four and will take you through how to win with a design-focused strategy. The other three focus on design, production, and delivery.

Service is ultimately about how you make your customers feel. Design, production and delivery matter. But they only matter as platforms on which to build the experience.

Value is defined as the customer's view of the relation between your perceived relative benefits and your perceived, relative costs.

- Design-focused organizations win by imagining new valuable things.
- Production-focused organizations win by making valuable things out of disparate elements.
- Delivery-focused organizations win by conveying valuable things from one party to another.
- Service-focused organizations win by valuably enhancing their customers' experiences.

While most organizations do some level of design, production, delivery and service, and all must market and sell, the most successful organizations have a clear focus on one of the first four areas.

Service Culture

A service-focused organization's main cultural driver should be flexibility. The front-line people interacting with customers must have the flexibility to meet their needs and exceed their expectations on the spot. Interdependence matters because the front-line people will need to leverage the rest of the organization to help customers. Purpose and caring matter a great deal in uniting all around customer service. But flexibility should rule.

Decentralized Organization

Decentralized organizations work especially well in service-focused organizations. This is inextricably linked to flexibility. Drive decision-making as close to the customer as possible.

The fundamental difference between a decentralized organization and a matrix organization is control of resource allocation decisions. In a matrix organization the geographic or customer-facing people share decisions with functional leaders. E.g. the Florida state manager and national marketing manager must agree on the Florida advertising spend. In a decentralized organization, the geographic or customer-facing people make their own decisions, like the Florida advertising spend.

This makes for faster, more flexible, more customer-experience focused decisions.

CEO as Chief Experience Officer

In an organization basing its success on its ability to create superior experiences for its customers, the CEO has to be the Chief Experience Officer. The Chief Experience Officer owns the vision and the values. They must live customer experience in everything they say, do, and are. If they don't fundamentally believe, they will get caught.

Just as Ben Hunt-Davis and his teammates evaluated every choice with the question, "Will it make the boat go faster?" on their way to Olympic Rowing Gold in 2000, the Chief Experience Officer should evaluate every choice with the question, "Will it improve customers' experience?"

Operate with Guided Accountability

Great customer service organizations operate with guided accountable. Everyone holds themselves accountable for how they make each and every customer they come in contact with feel.

Clear guidelines are critical. Think Goldilocks. Policies - mandatory, definite courses of action that all must follow - are too strict. Principles – ways of thinking about action – are too loose. Guidelines – preferred courses or methods of action that all should generally follow – are just right, freeing people up to act in the best interest of the customer with the guidance they need to make decisions on the spot.

If you're leading a service organization, both parts of guided accountability are critical to effective decentralization. Decentralizing without guidance is abrogating your authority. Guidance without accountability turns the guidance into theoretical gibberish. Only by letting people take up true accountability for the customer experience within agreed guidelines will things go the way you want. Though, if you've read this far you know that it's not about what you want. It's about what the customer wants.

The Stages Of Onboarding Into A New Job

Boris Johnson starting new job as Prime Minister of the U.K. Getty Images

Leadership transitions are some of the toughest challenges people face – professionally and personally. Nearly half of new leaders fail in their first 18 months. Often, those failures are the result of mistakes made in the very beginning that can be devastating for organizations and leaders alike. This is why onboarding is one of the most important crucibles of leadership.

This article proposes a framework for how you can take charge, build your team and deliver better results faster than anyone thought possible. It's about leveraging four ideas across the five stages of onboarding to get done in your first 100-days what would normally take six to twelve months.

The stages are before your first contact, and then between contact and offer, between offer and acceptance, between acceptance and start, and after your start.

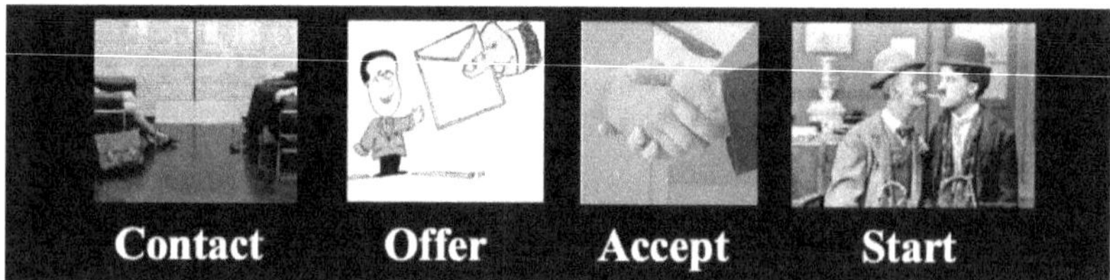

The four ideas are

1. Get a head start
2. Manage the message
3. Set direction and build the team.
4. Sustain momentum and deliver results

Before first contact

Those that wait until their first day to start their new jobs are well behind the curve. Onboarding begins before your first contact with any prospective employers. Before then, figure out what you want and how to position yourself.

1. Think through your personal likes/dislikes as your raw data.
2. Determine your ideal job criteria
3. Choose your long-term goals
4. Create options
5. Choose between your options by comparing them to your ideal job criteria and long-term goals.
6. Do a gut check. Write down your answer. Sleep on it. Look at it in the morning. If it feels wrong, you lied to yourself on your weighting of ideal job criteria.

Click here to request a free copy of our job search tips, elaborating on this.

The other thing to do before contacting anyone is to clarify your own positioning. Don't aim to be generally acceptable. Find the 90/10 positioning that 90% of prospects reject on the first read of your credentials and 10% have to have. You'd rather come in first 1/10 times and last 9/10 than second 6/10 and never first.

Between contact and offer

At this stage you're selling. Everything you do and say, including your questions, has to be designed to get you an offer. Prepare to ace the only three interview questions:

1. Will you love the job? (Motivation)
2. Can you do the job? (Strengths)
3. Can we tolerate working with you? (Fit)

Between offer and acceptance

Here, the tables turn. Flip from selling to buying and do a real due diligence. Dig in to get answers to three questions:

1. What is the organization's sustainable competitive advantage? (To get at organizational risk.)
2. Did anyone have concerns about this role; and, if so, what was done to mitigate them? (To get at role risk.)
3. What, specifically, about me, led the organization to offer me the job? (To get at personal risk.)

Pull your answers together to decide if your overall risk is low, manageable, mission-crippling, or insurmountable with the appropriate actions on your part. You may want to read more about our tool to assess onboarding risk.

Between acceptance and start

At this point you've made the choice – but you haven't started yet. There's a temptation to take a deep breath and relax. Don't do that. What you do next, what you do before Day One can make all the difference. So, choose the right approach for your situation, draft a plan, and get a head start.

- Choose the right approach for your situation based on the culture and context, assimilating in converging and evolving or shocking the system as appropriate.
- Draft a 100-day plan, mapping your stakeholders, thinking through your message, and then laying out a timeline for getting set up, jump-starting relationships, learning and working through day one, and your first 100-days.

After the start

Now and only now are you ready to begin:

- Manage your entry and your message per your plan.
- Get buy in to the one burning IMPERATIVE.
- Use key MILESTONES to drive team performance.
- Invest in EARLY WINS to build team confidence.
- Get the right people in the right ROLES with the right support.
- Shape the team culture with ongoing COMMUNICATION.
- Continue to sustain momentum and deliver results by adjusting along the way.

Why Steph Korey's Return To Away As Co-CEO Is Doomed To Fail

Away co-founders Steph Korey (L) and Jen Rubio Getty Images

Away company founder Steph Korey is breaking all three key tenets of effective leadership communication. This cannot end well. The basic mantra is Be – Do – Say, lining up what you do with what you say with what you believe. The way she led before she relinquished the CEO role is most likely her default way of leading. She tried to step aside as CEO and then changed her mind, leaving a whole lot of people confused. And confusion is not the goal of effective communication.

Korey got caught. She stepped aside and is now stepping back. But who she is has not changed. Her underlying beliefs have not changed. This cannot end well.

This is why Be – Do – Say is such an important thing to keep in mind in any leadership position and especially during crucibles of leadership like onboarding into new jobs or re-starting things. Start with who you are, what you believe. Then act that way. Finally, communicate both in your words.

Let's back up. Korey took her learnings from Kate Spade, Bloomingdales and Warby Parker and partnered with Jennifer Rubio to co-found Away in 2015. Their business success so far is indisputable. Adweek called them a "Breakthrough Brand with Ingenious Marketing." They primarily sell luggage direct-to-consumer while also having a couple of physical stores and their own travel-focused podcasts and magazines. The company was valued at $1.4 Billion in 2019.

Yet, that success has come at a cost. As described in the <u>Verge article</u> that led to Korey's stepping aside, she has a "fanatical work ethic." She's all-in with this venture, willing to do whatever it takes to satisfy customers, build the brand, and build the business. The trouble is that she required everyone else to be just as fanatical and pushed at least some of them way too far.

As Zoe Shiffer put it in the Verge article, "The result is a brand consumers love, a company culture people fear, and a cadre of former employees who feel burned out and coerced into silence." Not sustainable.

So, Korey brought Lululemon alum Stuart Haselden in as CEO and took the title of Executive Chairman in December 2019. Now, just 35 days later, she's reversing course and jumping back in as co-CEO.

This gets us to the fundamental problem. Her actions do not match her words and underlying beliefs. She can't help herself.

She said "her behavior and comments were 'wrong, plain and simple'" That reads like she believes the Verge article's allegations and needed to step away to change the culture. But now she's back. Actually, she never left. She just changed her title temporarily. She's always been running the company. She is still running the company. Expect the culture to stay toxic as she still believes that everyone should share her fanatical work ethic.

Lessons for you

Take Be – Do – Say seriously. Everything communicates. Everything you say and do and don't say and don't do sends a message.

Say. Your words are your first level of communication. People hear or see what you say and they form an impression. Words matter. Context matters. Think things through in advance so you're choosing the right words in the right context for the people you're trying to communicate with so they hear what you wanted them to hear and feel the way you intended them to feel.

Early on, Steph Korey certainly said all the right things. People partnered with her. People invested in her. People worked for her. People appreciated what she said.

Do. Words matter. But actions matter more. In the end, people are going to believe what you do more than they will believe what you say. If you're walking the talk, it's fine. If your actions reinforce your words, people will believe both over time.

This is where Korey diverged. She said Away's values were: "thoughtful, customer-obsessed, iterative, empowered, accessible, in it together." There's nothing wrong with these. But, as Shiffer pointed out, Korey actions and expectations were different.

- *"Empowered* employees didn't schedule time off when things were busy, regardless of how much they'd been working.
- *Customer-obsessed* employees did whatever it took to make consumers happy, even if it came at the cost of their own well-being."

Be. Even if your words match your actions, if they don't match your underlying fundamental beliefs, you're going to get caught - like Korey did.

January 14

The Secret To Seeing Around Corners

We all know them — those amazing people who appear to be able to see around corners. They almost always seem to know what's coming before anyone else does and be ready for it.

Here's their dirty little secret.

There is no magic. They just spend more time with outside-in thinking than the rest of us. They are constantly looking for potential changes and asking themselves, "What if?"

Thus, when things happen that surprise others, they've already thought through their options.

Peeking around the corner ullstein bild via Getty Images

Outside-in thinking

Premise #1: You can't control external events. All you can control is how you react to those events.

Premise #2: People needing to react quickly to external events have less time to think things through than those that anticipate possible external events.

Putting those together suggests you're going to better off thinking about possible external events in advance.

The 5Cs framework is a good place to start: <u>Customers, Collaborators, Capabilities, Competitors, Conditions</u>

Conditions: The context in which you, your customers, collaborators and competitors work in. Look at social/demographic, political/government/regulatory, micro and macro-economic context and trends and market definitions, inflows, outflows, substitutes and trends – as well as the impact of climate change on your organization.

Ask what if some of those change in ways different than you expect.

Customers: Those that benefit from the output of your work product.

Collaborators: Those that work with you to produce or enhance the design, development, selling, distribution or support of your work product.

Competitors: Those that create anything that your customers might choose instead of your work product.

For customers, collaborators, and competitors, focus your what if questions on possible changes in their needs, hopes, preference, commitment, strategies, and price/value perspective at any stage along their chain – including influencers.

Capabilities: Your own organizational strengths that enable the design, development, selling, distribution or support/service of your work product.

Of course, everyone you offer jobs to will accept and none of your key people will ever leave. Of course, all your people will deliver on all their commitments. But, just in case, ask what if things don't happen exactly as planned.

Range forecasting can help you understand people's 80% confidence ranges and prepare for different scenarios. There are differences between 1) will ship on March 3 and 80% confidence ranges of 2) March 3-10 and 3) April 27-March 3.

What? So What? Now What?

Essentially, your outside-in 5Cs probing and "What if?" questions drive you to think about more scenarios, complicating your thinking by choice. The what/so what/now what framework can help you sort through that mess.

"What" generally refers to facts. In this case, it refers to the possible scenarios you've identified. You're not pretending to know what's around the corners. You're just thinking through what could be around the corners. Get all the scenarios on the table.

"So what" generally gets at opinions and conclusions drawn from the data or scenarios. Sort through the scenarios. Do your analysis Add your insights. Determine which scenarios to prepare for and which to ignore.

Here's where the "How stupid would we feel?" question comes in to play. Ask how stupid you would feel if each scenario came to pass and you weren't ready. Then focus on the ones that would make you feel most stupid if you did not prepare.

"Now what" turns those opinions and conclusions into potential actions. This is how you get everyone ready to react to the most important scenarios. All should know what to do if those scenarios play out so they can move directly to action.

In many ways, the difference between a crisis and an opportunity is how well you're prepared to deal with it. Victims get surprised and can't react. Not you. You'll be ready to lead the way forward.

Take a strategic approach to risk management, mapping changes on a major vs. minor and temporary vs. enduring axes and then downplaying minor & temporary changes, evolving through minor & enduring changes, managing major & temporary changes, and hitting restarts for major & enduring changes.

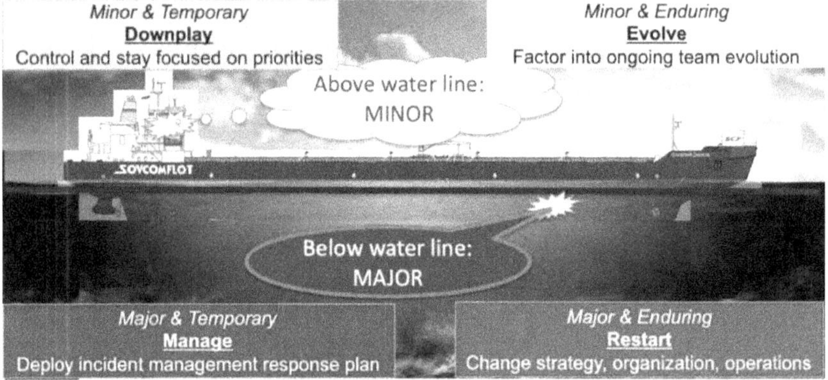

For major & temporary changes, deploy your incident management response plans that you prepared in advance. The reason you prepared is so that you all can react quickly and flexibility to the situation you face. Don't over-think this. Do what you prepared to do. Then bridge situational gaps to respond even better and learn from what happened to prepare even better for whatever comes around the next corner.

January 21

The Pillars Of Interpersonal Leadership – Structure, Leverage And Confidence

Martin Luther King - Getty Images

Interpersonal leadership is about inspiring and enabling others to do their absolute best together to realize a meaningful and rewarding shared purpose. While the most effective strategic leaders think outside-in, the best interpersonal leaders take an inside-out approach to people. They enable others by giving them a structure or framework to guide their own thinking and action. They give or get them leverage to accelerate progress. And they give them confidence in their own motivation and strengths to fuel the spark of inspiration that's already inside of them.

As I've written here before, the world needs three types of leaders – artistic, scientific, and interpersonal. Artistic leaders inspire by influencing feelings. Scientific leaders guide and inspire by influencing knowledge with their thinking and ideas. Interpersonal leaders, the focus of this particular article, lead other people.

The definition of leadership in the first sentence of this article is rooted in happiness. Happiness is good – actually three goods: doing good for others, doing things you are good at and doing good for you. Here are the connections:

- "meaningful" shared purpose – good for others
- "absolute best" – good at it
- "rewarding" shared purpose – good for you

The challenge for interpersonal leaders is how to inspire and enable people to realize that together.

Take an inside-out approach to people. This is the opposite of the BRAVE approach which goes outside-in, moving from environment through values, attitudes and relationships to behaviors. Don't get me wrong. Think outside-in. But lead interpersonally inside-out, starting with what really matters to the people you're leading. They're not going to be inspired by what matters to you. They're going to be inspired by what matters to them. (Oh-by-the-way, the closer what matters to them matches what matters to you, the stronger your bond will be.)

Starting with that, then focus on structure, leverage, and confidence.

Structure/Frameworks

People appreciate some structure. While too much structure is stifling, just enough structure actually frees them to act within boundaries. Frameworks are the basic conceptual structures that people use to flesh out their ideas. They help people know where to start, and they focus and guide thinking about how to achieve purpose.

For example, jury instructions give juries frameworks for their thinking. As US Legal explains, a trial judge gives the jury instructions to "apply the law to the facts as he gives it to them; they are not to substitute their own judgment as to whether a different law should be applied or whether the law as has been explained to them is unjust."

Frameworks are swim lanes for thinking. Use them to focus people on what matters most and enable thinking within boundaries.

Leverage

As an interpersonal leader, one of the best ways you can enable others is by giving or getting them leverage. Sometimes you are the leverage, helping them think or act. Other times you're a conduit for leverage, helping them assemble the resources they need to get done what they need to get done.

In either case, the key is not disempowering them. Once you've given someone else accountability for something, they are in charge. You should act as their first, best assistant. You're their leverage. They're not yours anymore.

Confidence

"They can because they think they can." Virgil.

Interpersonal leadership is not about earning peoples' confidence in you. It's about helping them have confidence in themselves. True inspiration comes from within. The things that are going to inspire others are already there. You just have to help them cut away the distractions to find those things.

Then, enabling is all about helping people recognize, understand and believe in their own strengths while helping them bridge their gaps. Trying to fix their gaps is generally a losing proposition and always a blow to their confidence. On the other hand, finding ways to take those gaps off the table by compensating for them allows people to focus on their strengths. It works better and it builds confidence.

Now you can inspire and enable others to do their absolute best together to realize a meaningful and rewarding shared purpose with confidence.

Why The P.S. Is So Important For Introverts

Extroverts vs. Introverts Getty Images

Let's start with the premise that you want everyone's best ideas – whether or not you choose to accept or act on them. Let's further presume that you have meetings for participants to learn, contribute and decide. The problem is that meetings, by definition, are geared to extroverts and run the risk of leaving introverts behind. If you want the best ideas for introverts you must, must, must, give them things to mull over in advance and must give them a chance to weigh in after the meeting close with a p.s. with the rest of their ideas – and often, their best ideas.

Extroverts like me think with our mouths. We do best ratcheting up good ideas while sparring with other extroverts. We're happy to float really bad ideas to prompt a discussion and debate so others can come up with better ideas in turn prompting our own better ideas, their even better ideas, our even better ideas and so on. Extroverts feed off each other.

I'm told (though I personally find it hard to understand how this is possible) that introverts think with their brains. They like to absorb information and then let it bounce around in their heads until it emerges as fully-formed ideas.

All kidding aside, you need both. You need everyone's best ideas – however they got there.

Now do you see the problem with meetings? Almost inevitably, the first people to open their mouths on any topic will be the extroverts. The second people to chime in will be…. other extroverts. The extroverts will bounce off each other leaving no air space for the introverts.

A skilled leader or facilitator will try to bring the introverts into the conversation at some point. But it won't work. The information coming out of the mouths of the extroverts will be bouncing around in the introverts' heads like unpopped kernels of popcorn not yet ready to see the light of day.

You've got to give introverts a chance to pre-think their ideas. (Pre-pop their popcorn?) Do this by giving them pre-reads in advance with enough information to prompt their thinking. Tell them what the main topics of conversation are going to be so they can mull things over in advance. This way they'll be ready to share their ideas in the company of extroverts.

How do you know in advance which are the introverts and which are the extroverts? The bad news is that it's hard to tell on the margins. The good news is that it doesn't matter. Send everyone the pre-reads. The introverts will love it. They'll dig into the pre-reads and be ready for the meeting. The extroverts won't pay any attention to it. They'll wait to engage with others in the meeting. This way, both will be ready to contribute to their fullest potential.

Click here for a list of my Forbes articles (of which this is #612) and a summary of my book on executive onboarding: The New Leader's 100-Day Action Plan.

P.S.

Don't forget the P.S. There's no way for the introverts to get the benefit of extroverts' thinking before the meeting. This is because the extroverts do their best thinking and make their best contributions in the company of others. This means there will be new information bouncing around inside introverts' heads. They need time to process that.

Hence the P.S. Give everyone a chance to contribute even more ideas after the meeting closes. Do this with an invitation in the final notes.

Putting this all together gets to the following basic steps for a meeting.

Prelude:

- One person responsible.
- Single overall objective set.
- Agenda set with clear expectations for learning, contributions and decisions by item, with time allocated to match what's needed.

- Attendees include those needed and no one else (with substitutes allowed for those who can't make it).
- Appropriate pre-work, analysis, and pre-reading to people far enough in advance for all to learn/contribute to their fullest potential.

Delivery/Moment of Impact:

- Meeting participation and timing facilitated to optimize learning, contributions, and action-oriented decisions, ending when overall objective is achieved.

Follow-through:

- Meeting notes out promptly to memorialize decisions and actions, inviting other ideas to improve best current thinking, and kicking off the preparation for the next meeting.

January 28

Onboarding Digital Natives Into Executive Roles

Young leaders Corbis via Getty Images

Executive onboarding is the process of *acquiring, accommodating, assimilating,* and *accelerating* new executives to improve productivity and retention, and accelerate results. The prerequisite to successful executive onboarding is getting your organization *aligned* around needs and roles. For digital natives born after 1980 and moving into executive roles, onboarding should be anticipatory, proffered, on-demand, real-time, personalized, collaborative, and bite-sized - step-by-step.

ALIGN: Make sure your organization agrees on the need for and delineation of the executive roles you seek to fill.

Start by stopping to reconfirm your organization's purpose, priorities and desired results, and how your new executives will contribute. Map out your message to stakeholders and candidates. Play those out in your recruiting briefs, current best thinking on executive onboarding plans and timelines; and align key players.

ACQUIRE: Identify, recruit, select, and get people to join the team.

Take charge of the executive acquisition process by creating and implementing plans with targets, timelines and milestones. Live your employment brand every step of the way. Assemble deep slates of strong candidates all at the same time. With options, you won't feel you have to close the sale with your lead candidates if it's not 100% right for everyone.

The way you handle offers and support your potential executives' due diligence efforts will impact the way they feel about you and your organization. You want them to say yes if it's the right move for them, their supporters, and the organization over time. You want a "no, thanks" if it's not.

ACCOMMODATE: Give new executives the tools they need to do the work.

Co-creating personal onboarding plans starts your working relationships. Collaborate to think through their jobs, deliverables, stakeholders, messages, pre-start and day one plans. Document 100-day action plans, and clarify who will do what next and how you're going to support your new executives.

Follow these first sessions with bite-sized, step-by-step interventions. Deliver a series of messages by text or other digital channels to prompt your new executives' thinking, learning and actions at various points. Don't assume they know what to do. By definition, they are new. At the same time, be ready to provide more depth on those prompts and help them in other ways — as they ask.

How you make new executive announcements influences how welcome, valued and valuable your new executives feel. Map the stakeholders. Clarify the message. Decide whom should hear what, when, flowing from those emotionally impacted to those directly impacted to those indirectly impacted.

Concurrently, accommodate your new executives' work needs (desks, phones, computers, IDs, payroll, forms, etc.) and personal needs. (family moves, housing, schools, etc.)

Then, prepare first days that put your new executives in the best possible positions. Everything communicates. Pay attention to what people hear, see, and believe, prompting your new executives with your advice and perspective. At the same time, pay attention to the impact your organization makes on new executives and on those supporting and influencing them - including their families.

ASSIMILATE: Help them join with others so they can do the work together.

Assimilation well makes things far easier. Getting it wrong triggers relationship risks. Beyond basic orientation, set up onboarding conversations for your new executives with members of their formal and informal/shadow networks. Do periodic check-ins with those networks. If there are issues, you want to know about them early, so you can help your new executives adjust.

ACCELERATE: Help them and their team deliver better results faster.

Make sure your new executives have the resources and support they need to put in place the building blocks of high performing teams:

- What most needs to be accomplished strategically (in place by day 30)
- Tactical clarity around what's getting done, by when, by whom (by day 45)
- One or two strongly symbolic early wins (identified by day 60, delivered by month six)
- The right people in the right roles with the right support (by day 70)
- Communication plans implemented on an ongoing basis.

Don't leave them hanging. Follow up with ongoing, periodic prompts and support.

Leadership is about inspiring and enabling others. How you handle the acquisition, accommodation, assimilation and acceleration of new employees and new executives, whether they are digital natives or not, communicates volumes to everyone. In many ways, this is one of the acid tests of leadership.

The Only Way Limited Founder Les Wexner's Successor Can Succeed

Les Wexner Getty

Taking over from the founder is always tough. Taking over from The Limited's founder Leslie Wexner after his 57 years as CEO is probably a fool's errand. The only possible path for someone to succeed must involve 1) Looking at the business context with fresh eyes; 2) Understanding what really matters and why to the organization, 3) Finding and leveraging the organization's special skills to win again, 4) Honoring and then building on the founder's relationships, 5) Focusing all on future impact.

Look at the business context with fresh eyes

Recent results indicate Wexner was wrong to stick with his faith in shopping malls as long as he has. His thinking that "people crave social interaction and will seek it at places like malls" no longer holds water. Shopping malls are in desperate shape and, as Investor's Business Daily reports, L Brands' stock "has fallen for four straight years, including 29% in 2019. Not coincidentally, L Brands earnings have fallen for four straight years, and it's set to cap a fifth straight decline when it reports fiscal Q4 and full-year 2020 results."

Understand what really matters and why

One good way to understand what really matters and why to an organization is to probe the founder's intent. What were they thinking? Did they see a problem they could solve? An unmet need? A gap in the market? Were they trying to carve out a living? One of the benefits Wexner's successor is going to have is that they can ask him directly.

The generally accepted story is that Wexner did an item-by-item profit analysis of the products in his parents' clothing store. He saw that higher-priced clothing like jackets had higher margins per item and lower turns. Conversely, lower-priced items like blouses, had lower margins, turned faster, and were more profitable overall. Based on that insight, he started his store with a limited selection of items that turned quickly and called it "The Limited."

Find and leverage special skills

L Brands has been in decline. But it's still a $6B+ business. It has some core strengths. The new leader has to figure out how to win by refocusing the organization as a designer, producer, distributor or service company. That fundamental strategic choice will guide everything else they have to do to accelerate through a point of inflection.

Honor and then build on the founder's relationships

One of L Brands' greatest strengths has to be the network of relationships Wexner has built over his 57 years as CEO. He needs to transition those to his successor.

One of the best examples of this was how Herbert Mines onboarded Hal Reiter as CEO of his executive search firm. They agreed an overall purchase price for the company with 25% getting transferred on Hal's joining as President, 50% getting transferred five years later when Hal took over as CEO, and the final 25% getting transferred five years after that.

Mines did such a great job transitioning his relationships and Reiter did such a great job following through and building on them that when they met for lunch to transfer the final 25%, Mines said "If I'd know how much value you were going to create, I would have negotiated a higher price." Reiter replied, "Let's do that now" and paid him more than he had to as a sign of appreciation.

Focus all on future impact

Yes, Wexner's replacement gets to and needs to stand on the shoulders of an industry giant. Yes, they need to do all I've suggested so far. But it's all theoretical gibberish unless the new leader focuses the entire organization on the future and deliver real impact.

L Brands' business context is terrifying. What mattered to Wexner when he founded the firm may not matter anymore. It's not clear L Brands has a sustainable competitive advantage. Many of Wexner's relationships are from the last century. Wexner's replacement's task is daunting.

They need to learn everything, understand the parts, and then rearrange them in a way that is fit not for current purpose, but fit for future purpose. Wexner's had an amazing run. It's past time for him to pass the baton to someone who can take the business forward.

February 4

The Most Important Choice Facing IBM's New CEO Arvind Krishna

Arvind Krishna Getty

New IBM CEO Arvind Krishna is going to continue to drive IBM's cloud business. That choice has already been made. The choice he faces is how best to do that. The answer is probably cloud as service – for the moment.

Ginni Rometty started moving IBM into the cloud to make it more relevant, but didn't go far enough or fast enough. As Andrew Ross Sorkin wrote in the The New York Times' Deal Book, January 31,

"The company still relies more on slow-growing hardware and software businesses than cloud computing, A.I. and data analysis.

Shares in IBM fell 25 percent during her tenure, while those in Microsoft jumped 500 percent."

IBM is in trouble and in decline. It has been there before and recovered when Lou Gerstner famously led the change from hardware to service. Now Krishna has to catch up in the cloud. Leading through that point of inflection starts with picking a strategy.

Michael Porter's value chain insights taught us that all organizations design, build, sell and market, deliver and service. The most effective organizations focus on one of design, build, deliver or service as the anchor for their competitive advantages. They invest to be best-in-class in that area while accepting world-class, strong, or good enough in other areas.

The trouble with playing catch-up is that others have already staked out their positions. When it comes to cloud computing, Amazon is winning with a distribution-focused strategy. Microsoft is doing well with a product-focused strategy.

Krishna and IBM's choosing to try to displace either of them with their strategies is doomed to failure. This means Krishna has to choose a different approach. The most logical is cloud as service, building on IBM's current service focus. That gives them the greatest chance of success – at least until Apple designs a whole new approach to the cloud and blows everyone else out of the sky.

As laid out in my earlier article on what it takes to accelerate through a strategic inflection point, that strategic choice dictates the organization's approach to culture, organization, operations and what the "E" in CEO means.

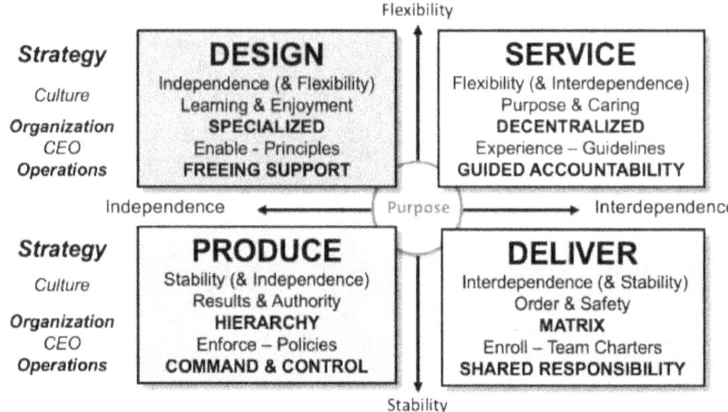

POI Framework Bradt

Culture of flexibility

IBM will need to evolve to a culture of flexibility (and interdependence.) IBMers will need to think "customer-first" and have the flexibility to do what it takes to delight customers. This requires interdependence across groups, all working as one to serve the customer. It requires fundamental mindsets driving purpose and caring about customers and each other.

Newly named President of IBM who was acquired with Red Hat, Jim Whitehurst, ran straight into this when he initially joined Red Hat. There he became a catalytic leader, but only after he was able to embrace the organization's unshakable focus on its mission. As he wrote, "The code talks."

Organization

IBM will have to become more decentralized, pushing decisions down and out so the people closest to the customer can make decisions in the best interest of customers (and IBM.)

Operations

The key to operating effectively in a decentralized, service organization is guided accountability. It's counter-intuitive, but clear guidelines free up decentralized leaders to make decisions. Knowing what choices they can and cannot make makes it easier for them to focus on the choices they can make and not worry about the rest.

The second part is accountability. If they get to make choices, they need to live with the consequences of those choices – both positive and negative.

Chief Experience Officer

CEOs' primary approach must align with the organization's core strategy. While situational leadership requires a fair degree of flexibility,

The CEO of a design-focused organization has to be the chief enabler, fighting to give the designers room to create.

The CEO of a production-focused organization has to be the chief enforcer, making sure the planes fly right every time.

The CEO of a distribution-focused organization has to be the chief enroller, bringing people into the eco-system.

If Krishna chooses to focus on cloud as service, he must be the chief experience officer, pushing everyone all the time to make their customers' experience with IBM's cloud superior in every way to any other cloud offering. The good news is that superior experience beats superior product and distribution – assuming the product and distribution support the experience.

February 11

How The Best Leaders Enable Confidence To Triumph Over Fear

Admiral James Bond Stockdale Bettmann Archive

Michele PW (Pariza Wacek) has reframed the Stockdale Paradox in a way that can help all of us. Her fundamental premise is that "fear is false evidence appearing real." It's crippling. The only way to conquer it is confidence – confidence in the real truth, confidence in our own feelings about that truth, and confidence that we can change things. Whether you call this purpose-based leadership, a love-based mindset, faith-based mindset, or confidence, it's a different and more powerful approach than leveraging fear.

Let's unpack that.

The Stockdale Paradox refers to Vietnam Admiral James Stockdale's approach to leading his colleagues through their time in a brutal North Vietnamese prison camp. He said,

"You must never confuse faith that you will prevail in the end — which you can never afford to lose — with the discipline to confront the most brutal facts of your current reality, whatever they might be."

Webster defines fear as "the emotion experienced in the presence or threat of danger."

Conversely, Webster's definitions of confidence talk about consciousness of one's powers, faith or belief that one will act in a right, proper, or effective way, and a relation of trust. We saw an example of that last week as Mitt Romney chose to honor his oath and faith and vote to impeach Trump, knowing he would not prevail over the short term.

Michele PW has put all this together as the basis of a mindset she deploys in own copy writing and book writing and work advising other online marketers and writers. She's interested in creating "love-based" businesses. When we talked, she made it clear that she was not referring to romantic love, but "the truth part." It's about "realizing what's real," and "not being afraid of our feelings," and certainly not "letting our feelings control us."

Her understanding came from her work as a copy writer. She learned that to persuade anyone to do anything, you have to tap into their feelings. A lot of copy writers tap into fear-based feelings like anxiety, guilt, shame, scarcity, anger, grief. Their argument is essentially, "If you don't buy our product or service, bad things will happen to you."

Michele gravitated to a different approach, leading from an attitude of abundance to attract, inspire and invite others to make the right choice for themselves with confidence. It's about respectfully and compassionately making others feel heard and understood with authenticity, honesty and personal accountability. While she started with copy writing, she's applied her frameworks to starting businesses, setting goals, and re-thinking business models, among others.

Often people's fearfully crippling emotions get triggered by something other than what is immediately apparent. As Michele explained, this could be some old grief, something in a marriage, feeling resentful about something else, letting their own dreams die. Whatever it is, it triggers a truth that people choose not to engage with. Instead, they sabotage themselves by picking fights, diving into non-productive busywork, or doing something else.

The antidote is to 1) understand the triggering events, acknowledging and appreciating the fears, and then 2) have the confidence to choose the right way forward, and finally 3) follow through to make your preferred reality true.

Understand the triggers and emotions

The point here is that you have to understand the triggers and emotions for everyone involved. If you're leading someone or trying to persuade someone to do something or buy something, you need to understand their problem and their pain. It's important to do this without letting it trigger your own pain or rushing in with solutions that would work for you, but not for them.

The right way forward

The "right" way forward for them may or may not be your way. This requires an "attitude of abundance" and being committed to everyone's needs being met but not attached to a specific outcome (such as making a specific sale). Make sure you're solving their problem, not yours. Don't push. Invite. If you lead with that attitude and confident authenticity, honesty and personal accountability, you will deserve their confidence as well.

Follow through

In a lot of ways, the difference between a transaction and a relationship is what happens next. Of course, you have to honor commitments and do everything you say you're going to do. But if you really care about others, you'll go well beyond your commitments to stay connected with them and help them progress well beyond what they ever thought possible with a new confidence in themselves.

February 14

How The Best Leaders Enable Confidence To Triumph Over Fear

The Consultant's Roller Coaster

Almost every individual consultant has experienced it. At the bottom of the hill, they put all their effort into selling. Then they get clients and head uphill. Then, at the top of the hill, they put all their effort into doing the work for their clients. Then, when the work is finished, they have no more clients and head back downhill to start the cycle all over again. To get off the roller coaster they have to be different, strong, and committed. Or, they need to be something else.

The five BRAVE questions apply: Environment – here to play? Values – What matters and why? Attitude – How to win? Relationships – How to connect? Behaviors – What impact?

Environment: Ask what currently unmet problem you can solve for your customers? If there isn't a pressing problem or someone else is already solving it well, there is not a business. Stop.

Values: Figure out why you care about solving this problem for this set of customers. If you're not clear about what really matters to you and why, don't waste your time or money. Stop.

Attitude: You must be able to explain what you do and how it is different from everyone else. Without differentiation there is no value. If you don't have that, stop. **BE DIFFERENT.**

This gets at core positioning: target, frame of reference, benefit, support. Get this right before you do anything else or you'll be competing on price. Focus on an unmet need or new way of meeting needs.

Relationships: If you can't connect with your customers, suppliers, allies and own people, you will fail. Teams beat individuals every time. **BE STRONG.**

Teams with Tactical Capacity beat individuals as they design, produce, sell, deliver, support.

Get a partner or ally so you can get better together, continuously selling beyond your own individual capacity and smooth out the highs and lows of the roller coaster.

Behaviors: Follow through. Relentlessly. Evolve your strategy as you learn. Evolve your organization in line with your strategy. Strengthen your operations on a continual basis. It never ends. Someone in your eco-system needs to be committed to designing, building, selling, delivering and supporting.

BE COMMITTED:

To customer satisfaction. It's why you exist. If they don't get value, you don't have a business.

To continuous improvement. If you're not getting better, you're getting relatively worse.

To business development. #1 job of a company is to create a customer. If you don't love selling, go do something else.

Every sales funnel that ever existed is based on some variation of AIDA: Awareness, Interest, Desire, Action.

<u>Awareness</u>

Planting seeds for the future is the top of the funnel. It's about getting the word out and building your database.

- Provide general assistance to people facing the problem you solve. Note this is about giving, not selling.
- Give talks to groups of people facing the problem you solve and to people supporting and influencing those people.
- Provide workshops and seminars to all those same people.
- Write, post, publish articles.
- Post LinkedIn comments, references, answers.
- Tweet items appealing to those concerned about the problem you solve.
- Comment on and forward others' blog posts, articles, Tweets, etc.

<u>Interest</u>

Water those seeds by starting conversations with people interested in what you have to say.

- Give out books – preferably ones you've written.
- Send out book summaries.
- Write and post articles and comments on your website and other appropriate websites.
- Connect with those in your database on regular basis through ETCs: excuses to contact.
- Explicitly ask for introductions to people with an urgent need for your help.

<u>Desire</u>

Nourish sprouts by digging into those with an urgent need for your help.

- Follow up on any and all requests for more information. These are calls for help.
- Offer your specific help to people facing the problem you solve. This is still giving, but setting up some sort of trial.

Support plants with momentum sales.

- Offer some sort of trial device that is valuable on its own and whets their appetite for more.
- Give more to those that really need it – and charge them appropriately.
- Over deliver on every assignment so people are surprised and delighted by how you helped them.

Or be something else. If you can't do all of this, look hard at joining a going concern, effectively paying someone else to do your business development.

February 18

How To Leverage Scouts, Seconds And Spies To Mitigate Executive Onboarding Risks

Lewis and Clark scouting the way forward Getty Images

As an executive onboarding into a new role, you don't know what you don't know. That's often an underlying factor when people don't fit, fail to deliver, or fail to adjust to changes down the road. If they'd only known the problem, they might have dealt with it. Build a network of external scouts and internal seconds and spies to help you understand what you're getting into.

Scouts

Scouts are external people with different perspectives. They could be customers, suppliers, allies, competitors, part of the community, regulators, analysts, journalists, former employees or anyone looking at the organization from outside.

These people are relatively easy to identify if you put in the effort and generally are willing to share what they know. Note they are – by definition – external and can tell you only what they see. They won't understand the underlying drivers of the organization's decisions and ways of working.

Leverage scouts to help you prepare for interviews, do due diligence, prepare for Day One and throughout your tenure to help you see things you might not see. Often outsiders see things that insiders don't. Scouts can help you see changes down the road so you can adjust as appropriate.

Seconds

Webster says a second is "2: one that assists or supports another especially: the assistant of a duelist or boxer."

It doesn't matter if these people are your boss, peer, subordinate, mentor or onboarding buddy. These are internal people that are explicitly assisting or supporting you.

These people can ask questions that you may feel uncomfortable asking yourself. Some people will tell these people things that they don't feel comfortable telling you directly, knowing the second will filter what they said and pass it on – sometimes with attribution and sometimes without. In any case, part of assisting or supporting is creating another channel of communication.

Leverage seconds both proactively and reactively. The ABC's of behavioral influence apply. ABC stands for Antecedent, Behavior, Consequence. People do things because an antecedent prompts that behavior. They do it again because of the balance of consequences: rewarding or punishing desirable or undesirable behavior.

So, if you want your seconds to identify things that could be going better, proactively prompt that behavior by explicitly asking them to do so. Don't expect them to do it on their own.

In any case, when one of your seconds comes to you with bad news, make sure you reactively respond in a way that encourages them to do it again. Not only should you not kill the messenger of bad news, you should reward them.

Spies

Spies are internal people who observe what is going on and tell you about it. Every organization has hidden back channels of information flows. I'm not suggesting anything hostile or inappropriate. I'm just suggesting that you make sure you're in the flow of at least some of those back channels.

If your new organization uses executive assistants, they form a natural back channel. Make sure your executive assistant is in that flow and shares things with you. In this case, your executive assistant is both a second and a spy.

One of my personal favorite ways of creating spies is to go three levels deep. After year-end-reviews are completed, get a list of your subordinates' subordinates' subordinates who got the top-box performance rating. Then arrange to have a one-on-one lunch with one of them each week for as long as it takes to get through all of them.

Read their review before lunch and say "I've read your review. You're doing great things. I asked you to lunch to learn more about what you do." Then listen.

It's a great way to recognize strong performers. They will feel better about themselves. It's a great way to learn about what your strong performers are doing and how things work.

And, it's a great way to build your spy network. After this lunch, these people will know you better. They will tell you what's going on. Your subordinates have a bias to tell you what they think you want to know. Their subordinates don't want to get their bosses in trouble with you. But those three-levels deep are too far away to be afraid of you. They'll tell you the truth.

February 20

Lessons In The Power Of Organizing Concepts From Last Night's Democratic Debate

Democratic Debate Getty Images

Last night's Democratic debate was a fire fight with verbal sparring in all directions. While everyone watching saw things through their own filters, it was clear that some of the candidates stayed closer to their personal messages and organizing concepts than did others. In general, those that did better in this debate were those that more strongly believed in their organizing concepts and let them guide their words and actions. Be. Do. Say.

Messages/slogans from the candidates' websites:

- Bernie Sanders: "Economic, racial, social and environmental **justice** for all."
- Elizabeth Warren: "Fight **corruption** head on and put power in the hands of the people."
- Joe Biden: "A battle for the soul of America."
- Pete Buttigieg: "It's time for a new generation of American leadership"
- Amy Klobuchar: "Bring people together, take on the major issues facing our country and to get things done."
- Mike Bloomberg: "Unite America, defeat Donald Trump, and start getting big things done."

Last year, Tom Porter recapped the winning US Presidential campaign slogans since 1948 and suggested that "An effective slogan will sum up a candidate's pitch to the country in a few words, and be powerful enough to cut through the endless onslaught of information in people's lives."

Some of the most powerful were not completely original. But they did reflect the candidates' fundamental beliefs:

- Donald Trump: "Make America great again/America First."
- Ronald Reagan: "Let's make America great again."
- Bill Clinton: "It's the economy, stupid."

It must start there. If the slogan does not flow from what the candidate fundamental believes, it's highly unlikely that all their actions through the years will have been in line with that slogan. With the intense scrutiny and opposition research of a presidential campaign, they will get caught – and called out like Mike Bloomberg did last night. He was forced to defend his previous support of things like "Stop and Frisk" and the way women had been treated at his company.

An organizing concept is the strategic core idea being executed in a slogan, message and communication points. Those with stronger beliefs in their organizing concepts find it far easier to stay on message. They're always communicating what they themselves believe and not reading PowerPoint slides or Post-It notes provided by others.

Bernie Sanders is always fighting for justice. Elizabeth Warren is always fighting corruption. It's harder for Biden, Buttigieg, Klobuchar and Bloomberg to stay on message because their organizing concepts are more amorphous.

The best example I've seen was Charlie Shimanski and his first gathering of the American Red Cross's disaster response directors. As Charlie told me for an earlier article - which you can read by clicking here,

"I start by getting a sense of what I want them to feel when they're done hearing from me - what I want them to feel, not hear me say....I wanted them to feel that they are at the core of what we do, that our success is on their shoulders. I wanted them to feel proud."

"Feel proud" was not a headline message. It was an organizing concept.

The most powerful organizing concepts guide slogans, messages, communication points to impact how others feel. Even though they are rooted in the candidate or leader's fundamental beliefs, they are not about the candidate or leader. They are about what the candidate or leader inspires and enables in others.

The first question anyone has about a presidential candidate or any new leader is "What does this mean for me?" Ultimately, all communication is personal. Candidates and leaders connect better with people that think those candidates and leaders can help solve the problems they most care about.

Those concerned about injustice or corruptions will gravitate to Sanders or Warren. The other candidates' messages may be too generic to inspire the same passion. Their paths to success lie in strengthening messages based on organizing concepts they believe in and others care about.

This lesson applies to any executive onboarding into a new role. They must craft their entry communication plan based on a clear organizing concept. That concept must match their underlying beliefs and guide their actions and words. Everyone they interact with will listen and observe for clues about what this means for them. This is true for presidential candidates, new CEOs and new first line supervisors.

February 25

When To Discard Your Loyal Opposition

Angela Merkel - Healthy debate Getty Images

You need a meaningful level of loyal disruption, challenge, rebellion, and deviation on a team. Without it, inertia sets in. You don't evolve. You stagnate and eventually get eaten by competition you don't see coming. However, when your loyal opposition ceases to believe in your purpose - your mission, vision or values – it's time to cut them loose.

As I wrote earlier in <u>Why the Highest Performing Teams Always Fail Over Time</u>, high performing teams need differential strengths, differential perspectives, deviation, and full spectrum creativity. You must find and nurture people with differential strengths that complement those already existing on your team, not reinforcing them. You must not push for perfect alignment of peoples' behaviors, relationships and attitude with your existing culture.

But there's no wiggle room on purpose. People that don't share your mission, vision and values need to go away.

Mission: Why we are here, why we exist, what business we are in.

There are four possible attitudes to your mission: disengaged, compliant, contributing, committed.

Those disengaged, impede the mission. They don't even pretend to be loyal opposition. They fight you and everyone pushing the mission either directly or passive aggressively at every step of the way. This is easy. Don't let them take one more step. Make them go away now.

Those compliant, do the minimum they can get away with to survive in the organization. While you should not expect them to help you evolve, they're not hurting you so long as they are doing tasks that don't require more than their bare minimum.

Those contributing to the mission are your most valuable followers. Nurture them. Encourage their differential strengths, perspective and creativity. Their deviations come from a good place and are designed to contribute to the mission.

Those committed to the mission are the heart of your loyal opposition. They put mission above all else. They will challenge any perceived misstep by anyone in the organization including you. Witness <u>Jim Whitehurst's onboarding into Red Hat</u>. He learned that people weren't going to follow his direction, even though he came in as CEO. It was all about the mission. He had to earn the right to lead. And that was a great thing.

Net, lose those disengaged with the mission; keep those complying – at least for now; nurture those contributing; and cherish those committed – just so long as they agree with the vision and values.

Vision: Future picture—what we want to become, where we are going – in which others can envision themselves.

Buying into the vision means accepting it as a worthwhile outcome of the work and effort to be done. Those buying into the vision share the same view of the organization of the future. They believe in the value of what the organization is going to do.

Still, it's entirely possible for someone to see how a vision is good for others, allows people in the organization to do what they are good at, and is good for the organization without that being the good they most care about doing, leveraging what they are good at or being good for them personally. They buy into the vision for the organization, but do not see themselves as part of that vision.

Net, those that engaged with the mission and both buy into the vision and envision themselves as part of it should stay – just so long as they share the values. Those missing one or the other should depart at some point along the journey.

Values: Things you will not compromise on the way to delivering the mission and achieving the vision.

On the one hand, this is relatively simple. If you won't compromise the values, you can't compromise on keeping people who will compromise the values. If you really believe in your values, the end does not justify the means.

On the other hand, it's hard to know others' real values. Of course, they are going to say they share your organization's values. And most will act in line with those values. But if they do not fundamentally believe in the values, they will slip up. Look for slip ups on small things. Learn why they slipped up. If the root cause is a different view of a value, make those people go away before they slip up on big things.

Managing Your Brand Through The Coronavirus Crisis

Coronavirus response AFP via Getty Images

By definition, a crisis is caused by a major, temporary change. Don't fall into the trap of managing the temporary crisis itself, instead of managing through the crisis. Of course, some people need to focus on figuring out how to stop the Coronavirus. And we need to give them all the support we can. At the same time, those of us stewarding brands need to stay out of their way while preparing the way for our brands to emerge from the crisis even stronger than before.

The suggested framework is to think in terms of physical safety, reputation and finances – in that order. The fundamental approach is to prepare in advance, react to events and bridge the gaps while keeping in mind that leading through a crisis is about inspiring and enabling others to get things vaguely right quickly, and then adapt along the way - with clarity around direction, leadership and roles.

The essence of the approach, per my earlier article on Learnings from Boeing's 737 Max, Coca-Cola and Procter & Gamble on Crisis Management, is:

1. PREPARE IN ADVANCE: The better you have anticipated possible scenarios, the more prepared you are, the more confidence you will have when crises strike.

Establish crisis management protocols, explicitly including early communication protocols.

Identify and train crisis management teams (with clear leadership and roles.)

Preposition human, financial, and operational resources.

2. REACT TO EVENTS: The reason you prepare is so that all can react quickly and flexibility to the situation they face. Don't over-think this. Let people do what they prepared to do.

Figure out if the event or issue is temporary or enduring, with a minor or major impact. Treat it as a crisis if it's temporary with a major impact.

Then turn your crisis management team loose to respond to the events. This is where all the hard work of preparation pays off.

3. BRIDGE THE GAPS. In a crisis, there is inevitably a gap between the desired and current state of affairs. Rectify that by bridging those gaps in the:

Situation - implementing a response to the current crisis, iterating through i) situational questions, ii) choosing situational objectives and intent across physical safety, reputational, and financial issues - in that order, iii) bridging gaps between the current reality and those objectives before going back to assess the new situation.

Response - improving capabilities to respond to future crises.

Prevention - reducing the risk of future crises happening in the first place.

This is recapped in our Crisis Management tool. Click here to get a free copy or download it from www.onboardingtools.com.

When it comes to the Coronavirus, start by deciding if this is your crisis. If you're the government of China, the Coronavirus is definitely your crisis now. If you're running a restaurant in the middle of Iowa, it's not your crisis yet. Don't weigh in on others' crises. But do be aware of what's going on, how it's impacting your customers, collaborators and community and be ready to iterate into crisis-management mode if it hits you.

In any case, get prepared, anticipate the scenarios, establish the protocols and your crisis management team. In particular, put protocols in place now to protect your team and your customers physically. With the virus' incubation periods, this is going to be about keeping your people out of harm's way, minimizing the risks of contacting virus carriers.

At the same time, don't wait until someone in your team or your customers get sick. You have to react to the virus' impact on those influencing your customers, its impact on your collaborators or supply chain and on the communities in which you live and work.

If you buy into this framework and priorities, the key choices are going to be reputational.

Putting people's safety first is not a choice. Do what you have to do to protect your team, customers and community.

Know you're going to suffer financially when the virus hits you. This is why you put money aside for a rainy day.

Ultimately, what you're going to be left with after the crisis is your personal and brand reputation. Re-look at your brand values. Make sure you are protecting your core strategic planks. Treat all in a way that enhances your reputation with them. Over time, they'll remember how you treated them and how you made them feel at the worst moments.

March 3

How Organizing Concepts Can Improve Your Interviews, Executive Onboarding, And Change Leadership

Organizing concept dpa/picture alliance via Getty Images

Organizing concepts are the connectors between your thinking and strategy and what you're trying to communicate. They help interviewers remember your most relevant strengths, motivation and preferences. They help you position yourself in others' minds as an executive onboarding into a new role. And they make it easier for others to follow your lead in accelerating through points of inflection.

I originally wrote about this the morning after the <u>Democratic Presidential debate in Las Vegas</u>. The difference between those that had clear organizing concepts like Bernie Sanders relating everything to justice for all and Elizabeth Warren fighting corruption in any form and the others who seemed to be trying to shoehorn disparate messages into the conversation was striking.

After today, we may have more clarity, with Sanders still focused on justice for all, Biden focused on decency and honor, and Bloomberg focused on competence. (There's another article begging to be written about which of those is more inspiring - perhaps after today's results are in.)

Interviews

There are only <u>three interview questions</u>: Will you love the job? Can you do the job? Can we tolerate you? At the same time, interviewers don't care about the people they are interviewing. They only care about what those people can do for them and their organizations.

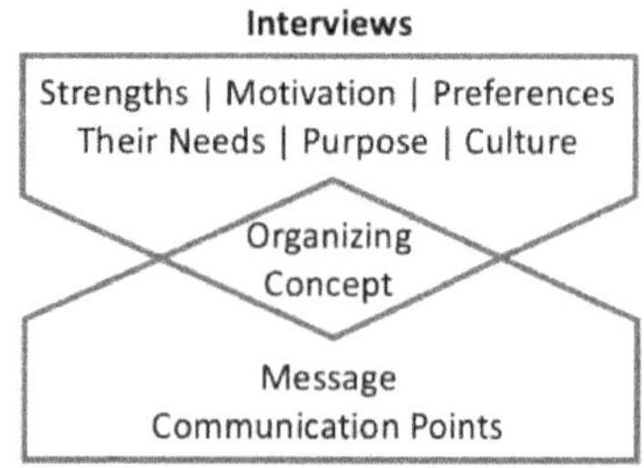

Thus, interviewing is about the candidate's ability to connect their strengths, motivation and preferences with the organization's needs, purpose and culture. The most successful interviewees, like the most successful politicians, are more focused on delivering the right message than on specifically answering the exact question asked. As discussed in my article on <u>acing the only three interview questions</u>, this requires pausing to think, answering the question asked briefly, and then bridging to the right message.

An interviewee's organizing concept helps them know which bridges are most important and helps the interviewer emerge with a cohesive picture of the person they are interviewing that they can explain to others – something like: "X is the right candidate. They perfectly blend a passion for our cause with the strengths and personality to make them successful."

Executive Onboarding

Just as there are only three interview questions, anyone meeting an executive onboarding into a new role has only one question: How is this new executive going to impact me?

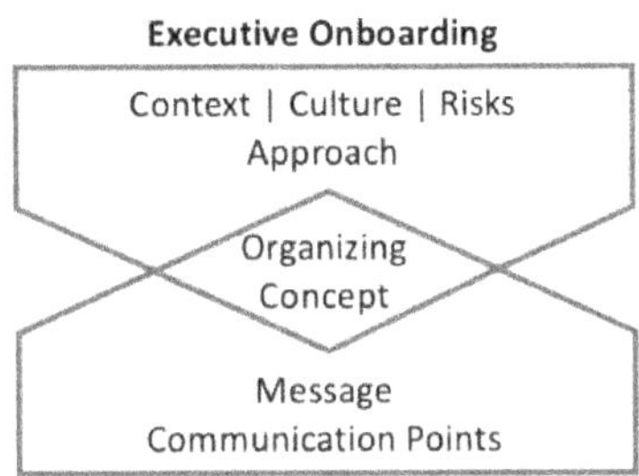

Executives successfully navigating the eight essential steps of executive onboarding will have thought through the context, culture and risks they face to determine the right approach for their onboarding. They will have landed on an organizing concept to guide their initial message and communication points.

The tricky piece is that as they are converging into the organization before trying to evolve it, they can't have a point of view. Any idea they espouse before they've done the right amount of listening and learning will inevitably and correctly be perceived as not invented here. By espousing any idea, they are saying they don't care what others think.

Thus, early on, a new leader's organizing concept guides their own questions, not answers. Everything communicates: what new leaders say and do and don't say and don't do including the questions they ask – like "How do we stay ahead of the curve?"

Leading Through a Point of Inflection

Change is scary. People facing change have the same question they have when dealing with a new leader: What does this mean for me?

Those leading organizations to accelerate through strategic points of inflection have to jump-shift their strategy, organization and operations all at the same time. They got to this point because of a change in their situation or ambitions and need to translate their situational understanding into a strategic focus, message and communication points.

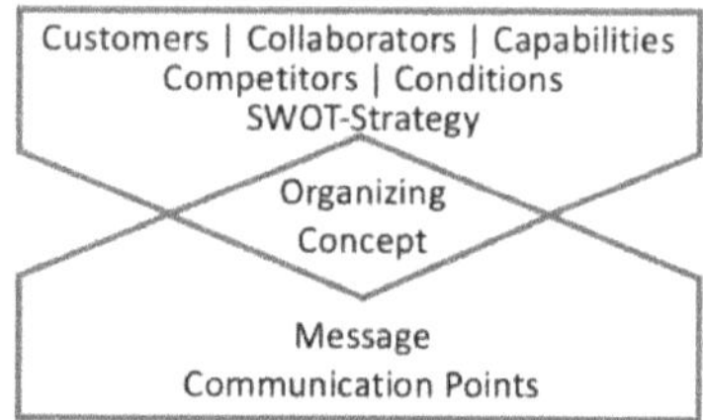

There can be an overwhelming amount of information for anyone to take in. An organizing concept focuses everyone on the most important ideas. It gives them a lens to filter and view customers, collaborators, capabilities, competitors and conditions on the way to building a differentiated strategic advantage. It helps them see how the culture, organization and ways of working have to change – like Jack Welch's organizing concept in his early days as CEO of GE: Be #1 or #2 in every segment or get out.

March 4

Leadership Lessons From Super Twosday – Relationships, Message, Resources

Biden connecting Getty Images

This year, Super Tuesday became Super Twosday and got the USA to a choice between two for the Democratic nomination for President. Kudos to anyone with the courage to throw their hat in the ring at any point. They each did the country a service by participating in the discourse. And we'll see more from many of them in years to come. The lesson from yesterday's voting is that people seemed to value relationships, message, and resources – in that order.

Relationships

Joe Biden is a flawed candidate. His stance on some issues in the past, the way he treated some people while he was in the senate, and his occasional speaking gaffs are issues. He was the front-runner and then stumbled on getting his message right and raising enough money to support a strong organization and media presence.

But he won at least nine of the fourteen states contested Super Tuesday. Tommy Christopher put it well in his last comment on Biden's response to the question "What drives you? What's your fire?"

Biden's answer was "Decency and honor and restoring this country's …. Everyone is entitled to be treated with decency and dignity."

Christopher noted that "Biden apologized for giving too much answer, but the exchange illustrated the essence of The Biden Show: freewheeling, personal, and overflowing with authenticity."

Biden won based on his relationships:

- People relate to that freewheeling, personal, authentic style. This guy's not hiding anything.
- People have known Biden for a long time. He's stood up for the middle class and unions forever. They relate to that.
- Key people jumped on his bandwagon after his early win in South Carolina. Amy Klobuchar's endorsement undoubtedly gave him Minnesota. Pete Buttigieg's endorsement calmed some nerves. Beto O'Rourke's endorsement had to help in Texas.

Biden seemed lost at the Las Vegas debate. Organizing his thoughts around decency, honor and dignity now goes hand in hand with his relationship building.

Message

Bernie Sanders message is crystal clear — "justice for all." It resonates with anyone feeling that they've been treated unjustly. Enough people in Vermont, Colorado and California buy into what he's saying for him to have won those states yesterday. Bernie builds relationships with people and has raised enough money to support an organization and the media necessary to take him through the race.

Resources

Mike Bloomberg has no resource constraints. He had 2400 people working for him in the Super Tuesday states. He spent ten times as much in advertising as did Sanders who, in turn, spent three times as much as Biden.

But yesterday, resources weren't enough. Not enough people connected with Bloomberg's message of managerial competence. Not enough people were able to relate to Bloomberg.

Summary

Rank Biden first on relationships, second on message, and last on resources.

Rank Sanders first on message, second on relationships, and second on resources.

Rank Bloomberg first on resources, and last on relationships and message.

Implications for your leadership

Relationships, message and resources all matter. While they are interconnected, think about them in that order.

1. **Think relationships first**. Always. The only thing any leader can do by themselves is to fail. As a leader, you're defined by your followers whether they work for you, with you or are competitors who join your cause. Think Be. Do. Say. Build your relationships on who you really are. Live your message. Then say what you think.
2. **Invest in your organizing concept.** Whether you are interviewing for a new job, an executive onboarding into a new role or leading others through change, leverage an organizing concept to connect your thinking and strategy with what you're trying to communicate.
3. **Assemble the right resources.** Strategy is about the creation and allocation of resources to the right place in the right way at the right time over time. You need to do this to activate your organizing concept and build your relationships.

Remember, these are not either/or choices. Biden, Sanders and Bloomberg did all three really really well. It's why they were the top three finishers. As a leader, you have to do all three. But at least on Super Twosday, there's evidence that relationships mattered most. Message mattered almost as much. And resources came third.

March 10

How To Guide, Not Make, Decisions As A New Leader

Bradt – Advertising Storyboard

The overriding prescription for your success as an executive onboarding into a new role is to converge into the team and organization before trying to evolve them. You can't make decisions while you're converging. You have not yet earned the right. Any idea you bring in and any decision you make while converging says you don't value others' opinions. However, you can guide others to the right decisions by helping them choose the right frameworks for thinking.

Per an earlier article, frameworks are the basic conceptual structures that people use to flesh out their ideas. In that article, I cited the example of judges' instructions to juries, telling them how to think.

In most cases, whatever organization you're joining already has a mission, vision, set of objectives and goals, strategies and plans. Together, those are the current framework for thinking and action within the organization. While, as a new leader, you don't have the right to challenge any of those pieces, you most definitely have the right and the obligation to help people to follow them.

Copy Strategy

On my first day as head of marketing in a new company, the general manager told me my top priority was to shepherd the production of new television advertising he had already approved to go on air before Thanksgiving.

I asked to see the boards (hand-drawn pictures laying out the frames of the television commercials.)

It was immediately clear those boards were not going to result in valuable advertising. But somehow telling the general manager that on my first day did not seem like the best way to endear myself to him.

So, I asked to see the copy strategy.

The boards delivered the copy strategy's benefit.

The boards had the copy strategy's support points in word for word.

But the look and feel of the advertising suggested by the boards did not match the character statement in the copy strategy.

So, I asked, "Do you think this advertising matches this character?"

He replied, "You know, that had been bothering me."

We scrapped that advertising, started over and ended up with advertising the built our market share +10 share points.

Learning

This worked because I was able to challenge the connection between the copy strategy and the work. I didn't challenge the copy strategy itself. I never said I didn't like the advertising. I just questioned whether they went together, knowing they did not.

Leveraging frameworks

Fit is not the same as congruence. Drive through that gap to guide choices. In the example above, the proposed advertising mostly fit the copy strategy. I leveraged the advertising – character gap to get my boss to decide to start over. His decision. Not mine.

Mission

Not everything everyone in the organization does is directly in line with the mission. That is how it should be. People do things that enable other things that support the mission. Sometime you can leverage that gap to guide different decisions. "Is this directly contributing to our mission?"

Vision

Vision is a future picture of success, by definition creating a gap with the current reality. Even if people are doing things that moves the organization in the direction of the mission, you can ask "Is this the fastest route possible towards our vision?"

Objectives

Objectives are general in nature. You can always ask "Is this the best way to achieve that objective?" Anyone believing in continual improvement will answer "No."

Goals

Goals are the quantitative side of objectives. You can ask "Will this deliver the goal?" If yes, you can ask "What would it take to over-deliver this goal?"

Strategies and Plans

Strategies are broad choices that guide plans. You can generally find gaps between them and ask if any particular strategy will produce a sustainable advantage for the organization or if the plans are the best possible implementation of any strategy.

Don't get me wrong. This is not meant to be a trick to drive your opinions before you've earned the right to do so. It is meant to be a way for you to pressure-check organizational decisions before you get to make them yourself. These are just questions. If people change their minds, great. If not, you'll get your chance to change the people.

How to Keep Your Team Connected While Socially Distant?

Home office NurPhoto via Getty Images

Keeping your team connected while socially distant is going to require virtual meetings. The better you can make those virtual meetings work, the more connected you'll keep your team. With the spread of COVID-19, keeping the appropriate social distance makes all the sense in the world. If you're leading a team, your top priority has to be to keep its members safe. Do that. And you also need to keep your teammates connected with each other to maintain and strengthen the team.

Meetings in which people can engage with each other with all their senses (sight, sound, smell, taste, and touch) will always be the gold standard. You can't really duplicate that in any virtual meeting. But 1) more deliberate content and flow planning, 2) a different approach to delivery, and 3) more, better, and stronger meeting facilitation will get the results from your virtual interactions close enough to those of live meetings to keep your team connected.

We are social beings. We meet to share knowledge, to work together and build relationships, and to make decisions and drive to action. Most will comply with decisions if they are made aware, even indirectly. To contribute, they need to understand through direct communication. But if you want them to commit, they have to believe in the cause, each other and in the decisions, requiring connecting emotionally.

Written words on paper, emails, messages and other platforms are generally sufficient to share knowledge.

Spoken words adds tone to the words, improving the quality of working together.

Live meetings are best for building relationships, emotional connections, and commitment to decisions as people breath the same air and communicate with words, tone and body language.

Virtual meetings via video, webinars, web conferencing, or virtual worlds can get us almost there with increased attention and investment in preparation, delivery, and follow through including:

- More deliberate content and flow planning to set up and prepare for the most effective virtual meetings' pre-work and breakouts.
- A different approach to delivery, doing more work before and after the meetings themselves, and in more and smaller breakouts.
- More, better, and stronger meeting facilitation given the process complexities to allow leaders and participants to keep their focus on relationships and content.

Let's dig into those:

More deliberate content and flow planning

The five steps to an effective meeting always apply:

1. Context. Understand the meeting's place in the broader journey.
2. Objective. Set an overall single objective for the meeting and clear expectations for learning, contributing, relationship-building, and decisions by agenda item and attendee.
3. Pre-work. Get appropriate pre-work and pre-reading to people far enough in advance for all to learn and contribute to their fullest potential.
4. Delivery. Manage meeting participation and timing to optimize learning, contributions, relationship-building, and decision-making.
5. Follow-through. Get meeting notes out promptly to memorialize decisions and actions, kicking off implementation and the preparation for the next meeting.

The big differences in a virtual meeting are going to be 1) more emphasis on pre-work and pre-readings to virtually eliminate presentations in the meetings themselves (pun intended,) and 2) more and smaller breakouts to enable conversations and co-creation.

A different approach to delivery

People are going to have a harder time sorting inputs and staying focused in virtual meetings than in live meetings. In live meetings, people can nudge them. Their attention gets revitalized by physical changes and changes in modes of delivery.

Co-creation requires people to be able to deal with multiple inputs at the same time. This is why it's going to be harder to co-create in a large virtual meeting. Don't try. Instead, let smaller groups co-create inputs into the meeting and then let the people in the virtual meeting contribute to improving those inputs. Interim pre-reads and itemized responses work well for this with people going through:

1. Questions for clarification

2. What they see as particularly valuable and

3. Suggestions for improvement

In that order.

More, better, and stronger meeting facilitation

Virtual meetings are harder to run than live meetings – driven by the increased complexities associated with people working from physically different spaces across different technology platforms. You'll need more facilitators. They'll need to have more skills. And they'll need to play much stronger roles in virtual meetings than in live meetings.

Taking A Stockdalian-Darwinian Approach To Your Business's Future

Bridge the gaps Getty

COVID-19 changed everyone's business calculations in an evolutionary instant. Some businesses will perish. Some will survive, but barely. Some will thrive. What happens to your business may have already been determined, or it may be the result of choices you make now. Choose to confront the brutal facts of the current reality. Figure out if your business can and should survive. If so, manage through the short-term crisis tactically while paving the way to the future strategically.

"Unwavering faith that you can and will prevail with the discipline to confront the most brutal facts of current reality." – The Stockdale Paradox

"It is not the strongest of the species that survives, nor the most intelligent, but the one most responsive to change." – Attributed to Charles Darwin

Together, they suggest:

1. Be honest with yourself and others about the facts of the current reality.
2. Choose from your possible futures.
3. Bridge the gaps tactically and strategically.

Be honest about the facts

Re-look at your 5Cs to figure out what has changed. Track the interdependencies. While COVID-19 is a health issue, it impacts almost everything else. How? Which are acute and temporary? Which are chronic and enduring?

Customers: First line, customer chain, end users, influencers.

Collaborators: Suppliers, allies, government/community leaders.

Capabilities: Human, operational, financial, technical, key assets.

Competitors: Direct, indirect, potential.

Conditions: Social/ demographic/ health, political/ government/ regulatory, economic, market, climate.

Pull all that together to understand changes in your internal strengths and weaknesses as well as external opportunities and threats. Crossing those yields your new leverage points and business issues. The existential question is whether you can leverage your revised strengths to take enough advantage of the revised opportunities to offset your revised weaknesses' vulnerabilities to revised threats.

Internal Strengths => **Key Leverage Points** <= External Opportunities

Internal Weaknesses => **Business Issues** <= External Threats

Choose from your possible futures

That assessment of your new leverage points and business issues informs your options. Can you and do you want to:

1. Shut down the business and do something else?
2. Jump-shift the business through a point of inflection?
3. Retrench and set a new base for future growth?

Shutting down the business and doing something else may be the right choice. If others can serve your customers better than you can, let them. If your colleagues and collaborators can do better doing something else, let them. If you can be happier doing something else, let yourself do it. Just because the business was viable yesterday, does not mean it's the best thing for anyone to be working on tomorrow.

If you're at a strategic point of inflection, re-look at and jump-shift your strategies, culture, organization and operations all together, all at the same time as appropriate.

If you're going to keep going, you have to respond to the changes and bridge gaps between where you are now and where you need to be.

Bridge gaps tactically and strategically

Normally tactics follow strategies. It's flipped when managing through a crisis. In those cases, you need rapid iterations through:

- Situational questions – what's happening and where are we now?
- Choose situational objectives and intent across physical safety, reputational, and financial issues - in that order.
- Bridge gaps between the current reality and those objectives before going back to assess the new situation in a few minutes, hours, or the next day.

You have to do that first to get through the crisis.

The next challenge is to think through and start implementing future capability plans at the same time. Then think through ways to bridge from your existing capabilities to what you'll need.

1. **Destination**: Start with the possible future you choose. Determine the human, financial, physical, technical and operational culture, capabilities, and perspectives that will require.
2. **Current state**: Do an honest assessment of the current state of those same human, financial, physical, technical and operational culture, capabilities, and perspectives.
3. **Gaps**: Highlight the differences between future and existing states.
4. **Prune**: Cut out people and programs that should not be part of your future so you can focus resources on those that should be.
5. **Develop**: Build plans to invest in and develop those that can be part of your future.
6. **Recruit now**: Determine which gaps to fill first from the outside and create plans to develop those new people after they start.
7. **Recruit later**: Determine which gaps to fill later and when and how you will fill them.
8. **Other gaps**: Determine how to fill financial, physical, technical and operational gaps.

Why So Much Of Crisis Leadership Is About Countering The Mood

If things are going generally well and people are heading in the right direction, deploy judo leadership, tactically redirecting their momentum. But if people are complacent or in a crisis, counter their mood, changing their state of mind and emotions and urging them on or calming them down so they can focus on what matters most.

Judo Leadership

Judo leadership is about half-full glasses. There are those that focus on the half-empty part and those that focus on the half-full part. You know whom you're dealing with their initial response to one of your ideas.

The half-empty people respond with comments that trigger fight or flight reflexes. They are perceived as challenges at best and attacks at worst:

"Needs more supporting data."

"Your conclusions aren't clear."

"Not sure that will work."

The half-full people make others feel supported. They lead with comments that open others up to whatever comes next – which should be even more support to redirect their positive momentum:

"What great research!"

"Terrific insights!"

"We can make this work!"

In a lot of ways, judo leadership is just this simple:

Think half-full. Or 25% full. Or 1% full. But focus on what's good, working, done right first.

Credit what's good, working, done right with a positive comment like the ones above.

Build on that with an addition. "And we could…" (Judo leadership is about "and" not "but." "But" negates everything that comes before it.) These should add value to what's already there with a modification, an additional benefit, another application, a new way to realize their original intent.

Check back to make sure you've preserved their idea. "Does this fit?"

Mood-Countering Leadership

Sometimes you need more than tactical re-direction. Sometimes you need a complete mood and mindset shift.

Counter complacency. One brand team had hit its annual targets nine months into the year. They relaxed. Their boss pulled them together, congratulated them on their accomplishments and pushed them for a plan to further accelerate their business over the remaining three months.

Counter stress. The primary role of leadership in times of crisis/disruption is to counter the mood with values-based conversations balancing "deliberate calm" and "bounded optimism" while demonstrating empathy and communicating effectively - maintaining transparency, clear expectations, and providing frequent updates.

Change only happens when A x B x C > D:

A. The platform for change – why they should listen to you and the subject seriously (ethos)
B. Something that helps them envision themselves in a brighter future (pathos)
C. A Call to action – things you can all do next together to be part of the solution (logos)
D. Inertia

Inertia and fear of the unknown are powerful forces. Mood-countering leaders must connect with people emotionally to get them to commit to a new path.

- If all you need is compliance, you can play at the bottom of Maslow's hierarchy and focus on what's good for them, indirectly making them aware of policies through indirect communication.
- If you need your audience to contribute, they need a sense of belonging and self-esteem. Play to what they are good at and build understanding by directly communicating guidelines through small group conversations.
- If you need their commitment, it has to be to a cause beyond themselves – something that is good for others in line with the organization's mission, vision, and values. This gets to the top of Maslow's pyramid and requires emotional connection to change their beliefs and mindset.

Mood-countering leadership

Connect emotionally. Start with why they should listen to you. Make it personal in a way they can relate to. Be authentic, relatable and vulnerable as you empathize with how what's going on impacts them personally.

Lay out the objective facts of the current reality in a deliberate, transparent, and calm way.

Paint a boundedly optimistic picture of the future – in which your audience can picture themselves. It has to be credibly possible.

Invite them to be part of the solution with a call to action including specific things they can do now. Be clear on the expectations.

Follow-through. This is not going to be a one-time event, but, rather, a series of iterative conversation.

April 2

Hot Landings: Starting A New Leadership Role During A Crisis

Hot landing Getty

Any executive onboarding into a new position should converge and then evolve. They should get a head start, manage their message and then pivot to set direction, build the team, sustain momentum and deliver results. However, if you're a new leader making a hot landing in the middle of a crisis, you must parallel process and: 1) Jump right in to help; 2) Learn with everyone else; 3) Let your leadership emerge over time.

In normal circumstances, asking for help onboarding into a new organization is a great way to show some vulnerability and start a relationship. In a crisis, everything is turned around. People are scared, confused and overwhelmed. They are going to appreciate you more if you come in offering help than seeking it. Be a team-oriented giver, not an individual taker.

1) Jump right in to help

Leadership is about inspiring and enabling others to do their absolute best together to realize a meaningful and rewarding shared purpose. In a crisis, Maslow's hierarchy resets and everyone builds back through the stages of physiological to safety to belonging to esteem and then self-actualization needs all over again. You have to deal with the current reality before you can focus on the future.

Even worse, as Harvard's Dutch Leonard explained in a recent session on Crisis Management for Leaders, in major emergencies like COVID-19, no one knows what to do. We're all operating in an environment with far more stress, far less capacity, and far less knowledge than anyone can reasonably handle. As he puts it, effective leadership is going to require "rapid innovation under stress embedded in fear."

Everyone's at the same disadvantage because no one knows how the crisis is going to play out or what the organization is going to look like on the other side. They can't help with your onboarding. But you can provide them needed extra capacity if you focus on helping them. Make it about them at the start, not about you.

2) Learn with everyone else

You've just crossed the border from Ethiopia into Kenya. You've cleared immigration and are getting back on the highway. What must you do next?

Change to the other side of the road. People drive on the right in Ethiopia and on the left in Kenya. If you don't switch sides, bad things will happen.

Similarly, every company drives on different sides of the road in different ways and you need to learn from others in the company how things work to avoid collisions.

But, in a crisis, it's like jumping into a moving car with a group of people trying to change tires while accelerating on a new road in a country they know nothing about. They're not going to slow down to give you an orientation on the rules of the road. You're all learning together. Don't ask to learn from them. Learn with them.

3) Let your leadership emerge over time

The core of effective crisis leadership is iterating through the following steps, all guided by your purpose (mission, vision, values):

1. Re-look at the new **situation and scenarios** from physical, emotional, reputational, political, and financial standpoints.
2. Agree near term **objectives** and **intent**. (Focus on physical safety first, reputation second, and financial implications third.)
3. Develop **options** for what you might do.
4. Predict risk-weighted **outcomes** for each option.
5. Choose which options to **prioritize** next.
6. For each priority, get clear on an **accountable** leader and what will get done by when by whom with what resources.
7. **Execute**, monitor and iterate.

In a crisis, all are trying to figure out what to do together. John Hagel suggests asking powerful questions is more valuable than pretending to have answers. Let your leadership emerge through the iterations as you learn more, clarify evolving roles and expectations, and earn others' confidence.

Think in terms of four stages: I) Listening and doing what you're asked to do; II) Providing input into the discussions; III) Making recommendations; IV) Making decisions – after you've earned that right through your work in the first three stages.

Timing your transition from stage to stage is going to more of an art than a science. Let the evolution of your relationship with your boss and team members guide you. Along the way and through every step, your communication should be emotional, rational and inspirational:

- **Emotional**: Connect with your audience, empathizing with how the crisis is affecting them personally.
- **Rational**: Lay out the hard facts of the current situation – in detail with a calm, composed, polite and authoritative tone and manner.
- **Inspirational**: Inspire others by thinking ahead, painting an optimistic view of the future, and calling people to practical actions they can take to be part of the solution - instilling confidence in themselves.

How To Onboard New Leaders In A Crisis

Helping onboard AFP via Getty Images

[Note this article is for those helping new leaders onboard into new roles. It's the other side of the coin from last week's article for the new leaders themselves: Hot Landings: Starting A New Leadership Role During A Crisis.]

Onboarding a new leader well requires aligning the organization around the need for the new leader and their role, and then acquiring, accommodating, assimilating and accelerating them. It's challenging under normal circumstances as 40% of new leaders fail in their first 18 months. In a crisis, you need to be much more disciplined and deliberate each step of the way.

Align

Start by thinking through how the crisis is going to impact your organization. Is it major or minor and temporary or enduring? Though, even if it's temporary, you can use it as the platform for changes to accelerate changes you should make anyway.

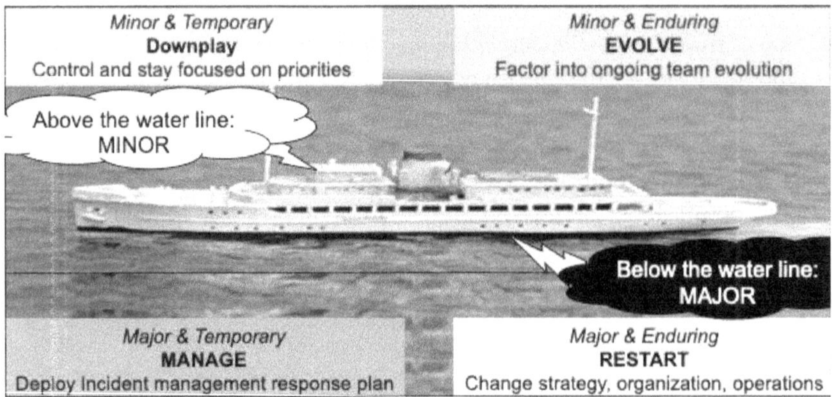

In a crisis, your new leader will be making a hot landing. This makes getting alignment particularly tricky. Maslow's hierarchy resets for everyone. All existing leaders and employees' first questions go to their own and loved ones' safety.

What you'll hear is "How can we add people when we're about to lay people off?"

What they're really asking is "Am I safe?"

Your communication about this – and everything in a crisis – should be emotional, rational and inspirational.

- Emotional: Be authentic, relatable and vulnerable as you empathize with how the crisis is affecting them personally and the importance of keeping them and all safe.
- Rational: Lay out the hard facts and possible impacts of the current situation.
- Inspirational: Paint an optimistic view of the future and how this new leader can help all get to that future.

Your objective is to convince all that adding this new leader is in their own best interest. (If you can't make that happen, either the new leader or some of the current employees or leaders should not be part of the organization's future.)

Acquire

You can't pretend to be one type of organization facing one set of circumstances while recruiting people and then surprise your new leader when they show up. Respect the people you're recruiting by laying out the hard facts of your current situation. If it's not for them and they're not for you, it's in everyone's best interest to figure that out as soon as you can in the recruiting process.

Play this out at every step of sourcing, recruiting, interviewing, evaluating and closing or not closing the right sale in the right way with the right new leader.

Accommodate

Make sure the new leader can do real work day one. Always important.
Even more important in a crisis. You can't afford extra baggage in a crisis.
Every tool you bring with you, every person you bring with you has to help
the cause every step of the way.

So, help them put in place their own personal 100-day or 100-hour action
plan. Get them set up physically or virtually so they can jump in to help on
day one.

Assimilate

Even in a crisis, you need to enable your new leader to work with others.
In a crisis, compress the timeline by helping them connect with people
even before their first day and setting them up to be helpful on day one.
This is about task clarity as opposed to role clarity. Give them something
to do – with others – that makes an immediate contribution. Yes this is
trial by fire. But set it up so the "trial" builds everyone's confidence in the
new leader.

A second priority in assimilating is learning. The bad news is that no one
has the time to invest in teaching your new leader anything in a crisis. On
the other hand, everything is new for everyone. Everyone's learning. Help
your new leader learn with others.

Accelerate

The ABCs of management apply: Antecedent – Behavior – Consequences.
Don't expect anyone to do what you hope they will do unless you prompt
the desired behavior and then reward it while punishing undesired
behavior.

Leaders onboarding in a crisis should move from I) doing what they're told
to II) providing input to III) making recommendations to IV) making
decisions. Prompt their transitions from stage to stage, pointing out when
they go too fast or slow and encouraging them when they get it right –
which they will with your help.

The Smart Steps to Reboot Your Business Post COVID-19

COVID-19 Pause Getty Images

Even when COVID-19's impact is diminished and the government gives you the green light, you still have to choose if, how, and when to reboot your business. The smart way is to reboot only the parts that can be successful. Then deliberately move through virtual steps before physical steps, over-communicating emotionally, rationally and inspirationally every step of the way.

If

The world is never going to be the same as it was before COVID-19. Assess what's changed temporarily, permanently, and fundamentally across customers, collaborators, capabilities, competitors and conditions - including environment, social and government as Neal Kissel highlights in his note on 5 lasting changes CEOs need to be planning for now.

Think through scenarios and your strengths, weaknesses, opportunities and threats, to develop a new view of your leverage points and business issues at this point of inflection and how those impact your strategy, organization and operations.

Use that to help figure out which parts of your business, if any, can and should be:

- best-in-class/superior to all other choices
- world class/parity with the top tier
- strong/above average
- good enough/minimally viable - and scaled or outsourced
- gone from the list of things you do - and not restarted.

How

You can't do anything until you can make, deliver and support your product or service. Ensure your supply chain, distribution ecosystem, and team are ready, willing and able to go.

Then, get ready to market and sell. This will require a reboot of your marketing/sales funnel. Everyone's world has been reset. Everyone's reevaluating their choices. Don't assume your customers will come back automatically. Instead, rebuild awareness and then interest, so you're in their consideration set when they desire a product or service like yours, and turn that into action.

When

New York Governor Andrew Cuomo put it well in his April 13 joint press conference with other Northeast governors. He said we should reopen, but reopen "With a plan, with a smart plan, because if you do it wrong it can backfire." He went on to say we need to "Take one step forward. See how it works. Then you take the next step." And everyone's plan may be different because the plans have to "fit the facts and the circumstances."

Andrew Cuomo AFP via Getty Images

With that in mind, think and act in steps.

Virtual steps:

Bring leaders back virtually to build out your strategy, smart plans, guidelines, parameters and practices – to guide everything that follows and so those that follow them know what to do and how they should work in the new reality.

Reboot or build supporting infrastructure and complete other tasks that can be completed without a physical presence.

Physical steps. No employees, allies, or customers should return until it is safe. Then use scientifically appropriate tests to determine which individuals can return to:

Prepare physical locations for other returnees,

Complete pre-start tasks,

Engage in limited reboot efforts to see how things work,

Reboot fully – noting not all have to come back physically or at all.

Communication steps. Wrap it all in emotional, rational and inspirational mood-countering leadership communication – as you should be doing more frequently than you ever imagined appropriate through the crisis and restart.

Emotional

Connect with your audience by being authentic, relatable, vulnerable and compassionate as you empathize with how the crisis has and is affecting them personally – Mayfield and Mayfield's empathetic language. As one of PrimeGenesis' partners puts it, "No one cares how much you know until they know how much you care."

Rational

Lay out the hard facts of the current situation – in detail with a calm, composed, polite and authoritative tone and manner. This is first part of the Stockdale Paradox. We're defining facts here as things that any rational person would agree are true no matter what bias or perspective they bring to the situation – objective, scientific truths as opposed to subjective, personal, cultural or political truths, opinions or conclusions.

Inspirational

Inspire others by thinking ahead, painting an optimistic view of a future they care about, and calling people to practical actions they can take to be part of the solution - instilling confidence in themselves with Mayfield and Mayfield's meaning-making and direction-giving language.

The optimistic future view goes to meaning and purpose: mission, vision and values. Ground all your communication in values: be – do – say.

The call to practical action is direction-giving, making people part of the solution, whatever part they are playing for their own and the greater good.

April 16

How to Make Executive-Level Interviewing Work Virtually?

Virtual interview AFP via Getty Images

COVID-19 has forced us to find new ways of doing all sorts of different things. Some are problematic. For example, interviewing executives virtually is paralyzing some. Senior need to fill open executive positions. But they and the people they are hiring are afraid to move forward without a live interaction. The good news is that all the needed virtual technology is already in place. You can make executive-level interviewing work well virtually if you:

1. Leverage the existing technology to work for you,
2. Pull some parts of a normal interview forward,
3. Make the interviews themselves as comfortable and fluid as possible.

Leverage the existing technology to work for you

You don't have to reinvent the technology. Your organization is likely already using Microsoft Teams, Google hang-outs, Zoom or the like for video conferences. And, with COVID-19, you and your teams have gotten a lot more comfortable with those technologies.

There are other options. For example, Harqen, specializes in video, voice, and SMS interviewing with tools that increase candidate engagement and compress the hiring timeline. They also have a live video interviewing tool that requires no software downloads.

In any case, don't let the technology get in the way. Haren's President and CEO, Tim Ihlefeld suggests having someone get the candidate (and you) comfortable with the technology in advance. Be clear which you're going to use, so they can download the app or program in advance. "Level set the expectations early and often – time, specific directions, software download – and how to do it."

Pull some parts of a normal interview forward

Ihlefeld suggests that the best executive interviews are more like conversations. And "good conversations evolve into other conversations." Enabling those virtually requires pulling some things forward so the hiring manager and candidate can digest them in advance.

Louis Hipp at DHR International makes the case to:

"Consider at least a part of your 'interview' process as the attraction part. Employed candidates will very likely be at least as uneasy as you are about making a career decision as you are in hiring them without meeting face to face? How do you get past this? *You* put in extra effort in the form of pre-work before each step in the process. You may have to write about the culture you are building, explain some of your history, detail your vision, make a compelling case why you must act now to hire this person, etc."

Ultimately, there are only three interview questions, ever: Can you do the job? (Strengths) Will you love the job? (Motivation) Can we tolerate working with you? (Fit) Set up the conversations by sharing:

Strengths

Strengths required for the job.

Other interviewers' ratings of the candidate's strengths.

Strengths, cognitive ability, sales ability, judgement, assessments done.

<u>Motivation</u>

The ideal balance of job motivation across good for others, good at it, good for me.

Other interviewers' perspective on why they think the candidate wants the job.

Any psychological, motivation, assessments done.

<u>Fit</u>

<u>BRAVE cultural dimensions</u> for the organization - current and aspirational (Behaviors, Relationships, Attitudes, Values, Environment)

The candidate's individual preferences across those dimensions.

Any psychological, personality, cultural fit, values, assessments done.

Make the interviews themselves as comfortable and fluid as possible

Start with motivation. Ask "Why would you want this job?" or "Hipp's starter question, "Tell me how this role might fit into your life right now." Have a conversation comparing what the candidate says with what you've learned in your pre-reading. Discuss any differences. Probe for what really matters together. As Ihlefeld suggested, "It's not about having alignment in particular. You want people to have different points of view. But all need to see goals and objectives the same way."

Then move to fit, with a focus on how they are going to do this particular job and relate to the culture and expectations. This is a great place to think through how to move forward together, looking at where the candidate would have to adapt to the culture and where the candidate can help evolve the culture.

Ideally, others will have confirmed strengths. Probe any lingering doubts.

Finally, put aside the assessments; look each in the eye (through the cameras;) and have as open, honest and transparent conversation as you can about whether or not you two believe you can be successful together.

April 21

Five Keys to The Decisive Action You Need to Accelerate Out Of COVID-19

New Zealand Prime Minister Jacinda Ardern Getty Images

The Powell Doctrine lays out five keys to using all the force necessary to achieve a decisive and successful ongoing result. The same approach works for you as leaders rebooting after COVID-19:

1) Get to the ground truth.
2) Set a decisive objective.
3) Concentrate decisive force at the decisive place and time.
4) Prepare your troops for success.
5) Be personally present at the point of decisions.

1) Get to the ground truth

Former Chairman of the Joint Chiefs of Staff and U.S. Secretary of State, Colin Powell, describes the need for leaders to know "ground truth." This is unvarnished, unfiltered truth about the harsh reality. Powell got his from chaplains, sergeants major, inspectors general and normal soldiers.

Get your ground truth from data, facts, and first line supervisors. They are close enough to the front lines to know the truth, one step back so they can see the forest and not just the trees, and far enough away from you not to be afraid of you.

2)   Set a decisive objective

A decisive objective at a decisive place and time is one which, if you gain it, you win - what Clausewitz called the "strategic center of gravity."

Ask the first two BRAVE questions, "What matters and why?" and "Where to play?" to inform your objective and first strategy choice respectively. Recent research by Marakon confirmed, yet again, that, "The path to superior performance is determined by management's decisions about where to focus the firm's strategic resources (time, people and capital)."

3)   Concentrate decisive force at the decisive place and time

Powell says, "Concentrate combat power at the decisive place and time," directing "every military operation towards a clearly defined, decisive, and obtainable objective." This is in line with the US Army's mantra of mass, objective, offensive, surprise, economy of force, maneuver, unity of command, security, simplicity.

In the first Gulf War, the US General, Schwarzkopf asked for one aircraft carrier battle group. Powell gave him two because he felt it "added to the insurance policy that would give us ultimate victory."

Jimmy Carter failed to rescue the US hostages in Iran and later said, "If I'd sent two helicopters, I would have been reelected president."

Countries that moved faster and more decisively on COVID-19 had better results. Taiwan, Iceland, South Korea, Germany and New Zealand were better prepared, quicker and more aggressive.

Ask "How to win?" The essence of strategy is the creation and allocation of resources to the right place at the right time over time. This is about concentrating your efforts to create a decisive advantage over your opponent – whether it's a business competitor or virus.

Identify your key resources and deploy more than you think you need when and where it really matters.

4)   Prepare your troops for success

"Soldiers given a task they haven't been prepared for lose confidence in themselves and, fatally, in their leaders." Prepare them and take the necessary time to get them ready to win.

This is about clear direction, bounded authority, resources, and accountability. Make sure your people:

- Know what's expected of them – the clearly defined, decisive, and obtainable objective.
- Understand what tactical decisions they can make on the way to achieving that objective.
- Have the financial, technical, operational and human resources they need to succeed.
- Accept their accountability to achieve that objective with those resources.

New Zealand Prime Minister Jacinda Ardern has done this particularly well, giving us a masterclass in how to connect through crisis leadership and communication.

5) Be personally present at the point of decision

The point of decision is the place where key decisions can make the difference between success and failure. Following through and being personally present there will allow you to adjust your plans in real time as "no plan survives first contact with an enemy." Strategy and planning are useless intellectual exercises until they are turned into decisive impact.

Darwin told us it's not the strongest that survive, but those best able to adapt. This is why, even if you've delegated accountability, you must follow through and be fully engaged at the critical moments. Ideally, you'll ask your subordinates, "How can I help?" You've put them in charge of achieving their objectives – until you need to change. When you do, don't hesitate to take back control and redirect resources.

Why Middle Managers are Particularly Vulnerable to COVID-19

COVID-19 is impacting all of us in ways we see and in ways we don't see. One of those is that we're all building new skills in working and managing virtually. That's going to mean that the physical presence of managers matters less and we'll need less span-breaking managers of managers – middle managers.

Recall Charon, Drotter and Noel's Leadership Pipeline levels:

1. Enterprise Leader (CEO)
2. Group Leader (span-breaker)
3. Business Leader (general manager)
4. Functional Leader (department head)
5. Leading Leaders (span-breaker)
6. Leading Others (supervise tasks)
7. Leading Self (front-line worker)

Every enterprise needs front-line workers who perform tasks. Those workers need supervisors supporting, monitoring and adjusting their tasks. Starting at the top, every enterprise needs an enterprise leader managing the whole and general managers looking across functions at the business unit level. Departments like R&D, production, distribution, sales, marketing, finance and the like need leaders with functional expertise.

But those managing groups of businesses or groups of managers exist only to make life easier for enterprise and functional leaders. The mass adoption of Internet-enabled communication tools has made it easier for enterprise and functional leaders to manage greater and greater spans of control. Now, COVID-19's social distance imperatives have forced everyone to learn new ways of communicating and managing. That enduring change will minimize the need for those middle managers.

It's not that the work of middle managers will go away. It's just that new ways of working will make it easier for others to do the work and manage the work. Think in terms of processes, programs, projects and tasks.

Processes

Enterprise and business leaders, whether their titles are CEO, President or General Manager, don't actually produce anything themselves. Instead, they own strategic, organizational and operational processes that direct and guide others' work. The most effective leaders engage with, monitor, and adjust these processes on a quarterly basis.

Programs

Programs get nested within processes. The 2021 Ford F-150 Truck is an example of a program. These tend to run for extended periods of time, getting monitored and adjusted monthly. Instead of having program-dedicated middle managers, assigning a functional leader as program manager can be a great way for that functional leader to work across functions and broaden their leadership skills.

Projects

Projects are the working components of programs, getting monitored and adjusted weekly. Engine design, dealer pricing and consumer marketing are all examples of projects within the F-150 program. Instead of having project-dedicated middle managers, having first line supervisors manage projects can enable them to broaden their leadership skills.

Tasks

Tasks are the real work of projects, programs and processes, getting performed, managed and adjusted at least daily.

The point is that others can do all the work middle managers are currently doing.

Implication for enterprises

As you're looking to retrench or shift your business in the wake of COVID-19, look hard at eliminating swathes of middle managers. Others can leverage new ways of working to manage more people and can pick up the work of eliminated middle managers.

Do separate the roles from the people. Accelerate promotions for your high performers ready to get promoted. Find other roles for your high performers not ready for promotion – perhaps having them pick up some program or project management. And help your poor performers ease into roles at other enterprises.

1. Take a hard look at your business and determine if it can and should survive. If so, determine whether your current strategy still holds and you can pause to accelerate, or whether you need to manage through a point of inflection, jump-shifting your strategy, organization and operations all at the same time.

2. Use that strategic re-look to determine which programs and projects are most important.

3. Re-deploy your resources, including middle managers, to those programs and projects.

Implication for middle managers

Be afraid. Be very much afraid. If your role is essentially span-breaking, it's untenable. Expect it to go away in better-managed, more forward-looking enterprises. And expect the less well-managed, less forward-looking enterprises to go away in their entirety – along with your role.

The only defense is to make yourself invaluable. Make sure you are contributing to projects and programs in ways others cannot do. And make sure you can contribute to future projects and programs by strengthening relationships, knowledge and skills on a continual basis.

April 24

What PG&E's Next CEO Must Do to Break Its Death Spiral?

PG&E sparked fires AFP via Getty Images

Fourteen months ago, California utility PG&E CEO Geisha Williams left incoming CEO Bill Johnson three envelopes on her way out and told him to open them one at a time, when things got tough.

He opened the first a couple of months in. Her note said "Blame your predecessor." So, he did, blaming "negligence by the company's past management for a cascade of catastrophes that killed nearly 140 people as he tried to persuade California regulators Tuesday that he is steering the utility to make safety its top priority."

His specific remarks were, "I think there has been a lack of accountability in the leadership to produce good safety results."

Things did not improve. So, he opened the second envelope. This note said "reorganize." So, he did, eliminating 80% of PG&E's top executives and promising to continue to purge employees "who didn't emphasize safety above all else."

This is not a new idea. "Every time we were beginning to form up into teams, we would be reorganized. I was to learn later in life that we tend to meet new situations by reorganizing... and a wonderful method it can be for creating the illusion of progress while producing confusion, inefficiency, and demoralization." - Gaius Petronius, Roman governor and advisor (arbiter) to Nero – in A.D. 65

Finally, Johnson opened the last envelope. That note said "Prepare three envelopes."

The three-envelopes are an old joke. But PG&E seems to keep doing this. Now Johnson is out after 14 months, adding himself to the 40% of leaders that fail in 18 months in general.

Californians can only hope Johnson's successor does a good, BRAVE job of resetting the organization's culture.

Let's unpack that. Leaders need conceptual frameworks to help them sort incoming intelligence and guide their decisions. They also help those providing intelligence to leaders give them Susan Gordon's "wisdom, clarity and insight" in ways that are most useful to them.

Three Goods and BRAVE Culture are such frameworks.

Three Goods

Happiness is good. Actually, it's a balance of three goods, doing 1) good for others, 2) things I'm good at and 3) good for me.

BRAVE Culture

Ultimately, culture is the only sustainable competitive advantage and BRAVE is a framework for thinking about culture.

- Behaviors: What impact? *Implementation*.
- Relationships: How to connect? *Communication*.
- Attitude: How to win? *Choices*.
- Values: What matters and why? *Purpose*.
- Environment: Where to play? *Context*.

The frameworks lead to the only way for PG&E's next CEO to break its death spiral. It's a classic "from-to."

In terms of "good," PG&E is a public utility. How can its mission be anything other than improving its customers lives' – good for others? Indeed, as Johnson said,

"As we look to PG&E's next chapter, this great company should be led by someone who has the time and career trajectory ahead of them to ensure that it fulfills its promise to re-imagine itself as a new utility and deliver the safe and reliable service that its customers and communities expect and deserve."

Yet, when he came in to turn things around 14 months ago, Johnson said he was "going to be pretty laid back." He negotiated a three-year contract with a substantial signing bonus and all sorts of things that protected much of his compensation if he didn't make it through the three years.

Culturally, the core is going to be purpose, choices and communication.

Leadership is about inspiring and enabling others to do their absolute best together to realize a meaningful and rewarding shared purpose. PG&E's current stated purpose is the "transmission and delivery of energy." Seriously? That's not inspiring. What's inspiring is how that energy improves people's lives. The new CEO needs to figure that out and rally people around that.

Strategy is about the creation and allocation of resources to the right place in the right way at the right time over time. Of course, PG&E has to stop burning down the state, blowing up communities and failing on a regular basis. But the absence of a negative is not necessarily a positive. Johnson's

"No more disasters, no more catastrophes, no more fatalities" was nowhere near good enough.

Everything communicates. PG&E's new CEO will be leading out of compound crises. Their leadership and communication must be emotional, rational and inspirational. Where Johnson went radio-silent after cutting off power to 2 million customers, the new CEO must be fully present.

April 28

Why All Should Tell Their Own Stories

Lunch and learn Fairfax Media via Getty Images

Filters are bad. Connections are good. If you remember nothing else from this, remember that. Anytime anyone is relaying someone else's story to you, it's getting filtered, diluted and polluted with their biases. Don't let that happen. Get to the source. Enable others to tell their stories directly to you so you have the best information, insights and feel for what's really making things work.

Intuitively, you already know that the real work is done outside the ivory tower of your executive suite. McKinsey has quantified that. In "The Mindset and Practices of Excellent CEOs," they note that "Of the 50 most value-creating roles in any given organization, only 10 percent normally report to the CEO directly. Sixty percent are two levels below, and 20 percent sit farther down."

Of course, the board and senior leadership should have approval rights for the major strategic decisions. That same McKinsey article starts by noting that "What the CEO controls—the company's biggest moves—accounts for 45 percent of a company's performance."

But those decisions are theoretically excellent and practically useless until they get implemented well. Enter middle managers two or more levels below the CEO. Any decision has influencers, deciders and implementers. The deciders make their decisions with the help of the influencers. But the implementers have veto rights and dilution rights. Every organization has its own passive aggressors. Indeed, you want thinking agents who question decisions they think make no sense and then implement the right things with their full commitment.

Get to those middle managers, directing the actual implementation of your ideas. They can make all the difference. If you're a board member, insist on getting to know the CEO's direct reports and their direct reports. If you're a senior leader, drill all the way down from time to time.

Get to the source

When I was a member of Coca-Cola's leadership team in Japan, I spent at least one day per month on a truck with a route driver calling on local stores. This kept me in touch with what was really happening. On one occasion, we'd made a couple of strategic pivots. We were proud of our ability to adjust rapidly to changing circumstances. Unfortunately, all that was changing were our PowerPoint slides. The route drivers couldn't keep up with the changes and were still implementing programs in line with three strategies back.

Build an internal network

One of my favorite leadership exercises involves top performers three levels down. Your direct reports have a bias to tell you what they think you want to hear. Their direct reports don't want to say anything that will get their bosses in trouble with you. But the direct reports of those people, three levels down, are too far away from you to worry about you.

The exercise goes like this.

1. Get a list of the most highly rated performers three levels down.
2. Arrange a one-on-one lunch with one of them each week for as long as it takes.
3. Read their last performance review.
4. At lunch, say "I read your last review. What amazing work you're doing! Tell me more about what you do."
5. Then, shut up and listen.

They will feel appreciated. You'll learn more about excellent performance in your organization. They will tell you what's really going on. And you will have connected with them on a whole new level. When they pass you in the hallways, they'll say hello – and tell you more about what's working and not working.

Tell your own story

This works both ways. Model the behavior for others. Don't let others tell others' stories to you. Insist on hearing them from the horses' mouths. And don't let others tell your story.

Square this circle by remembering that leadership is not about you. It's about inspiring and enabling others to do their absolute best together to realize a meaningful and rewarding shared purpose. Tell your own story about why the purpose matters to you and how you're going to help others realize it. Let others tell their stories about why the purpose matters to them and how they're going to help others realize it.

You tell your story. They tell their stories. No filters. Strong connections. If all help realize the same purpose, you'll get there together.

May 1

The #1 Challenge in Virtual Executive Onboarding – Making Emotional Connections

Making an emotional connection SOPA Images/LightRocket via Getty Images

In general, digital natives born after 1980 have done more communicating on screens than previous generations. (Duh.) Unfortunately, this has made it more difficult for them to establish emotional connections and trust with their non-digitally native colleagues - especially as executives onboarding into new roles. But now, all of a sudden, we've all gone digitally native and have to do a better job of communicating feelings and attitudes as close-to-live as we can.

Many are familiar with the 10-35-55 rule suggesting 10% of communication is in the words, 35% is in the tone and 55% is in the body language. Albert Mahrabian's actual study, which he described in "Silent messages: Implicit communication of emotion and attitudes," applied only to a more specific and precise case:

7% of message pertaining to feelings and attitudes is in the words that are spoken.

38% of message pertaining to feelings and attitudes is paralinguistic (the way that the words are said).

55% of message pertaining to feelings and attitudes is in facial expression.

This, of course, is exactly what executives onboarding into new roles have to do. They have to communicate and connect at a feeling and attitudinal level to establish trusting relationships.

Many digital natives have spent too much time in their formative years connecting through screens instead of live and face-to-face. They rely on words and substitute emojis for tone and facial expression.

We've all seen examples of this playing out with people coming in to lead or join teams. I was in the office of one new leader, four weeks into his role. He told me he had spent his first few weeks learning about the business, its situation and his team, and was ready to share his go-forward strategy with them. He explained this would be an education process because it was going to be new to all, so he was going to go slow, starting with a simplified two-page document.

I asked, "What are you going to do with that document?"

"Get my boss's approval and then share it with my team."

"How?"

He looked at me blankly, not understanding the question.

Do you understand the question and what was wrong with his approach?

"Educating" is the same as Bryan Smith's "telling." Smith lays out five ways to persuade someone: tell, sell, test, consult, co-create. The different ways yield different levels of engagement. Telling (or educating) yields compliance at best. If you want people to contribute, you need to sell, test or consult. And, if you want people to commit, they have to co-create and co-own the path forward.

The new leader in our story above changed his approach. His new plan was to:

Have face-to-face, live meetings with his direct reports and peers to get their input on his current best thinking.

Then have a face-to-face, live meeting with his boss to get approval to the strategic direction.

Then have another face-to-face, live meeting with his direct reports to share the approved strategic direction and co-create their tactical path forward.

Implications for onboarding those born after 1980 or who have been forever changed by COVID-19's social distancing.

Accept them as the digital natives or survivors they are. Use digital methods to communicate things they need to be aware of and comply with. Enable their digital communication in the same vein.

Prompt and encourage live, face-to-face meetings when possible for times when feelings and attitudes matter.

This is always going to apply to early meetings with new colleagues up, across and down where mutual trust is going to be important.

This is also going to apply to pivotal communication and decision-making meetings where feelings and attitudes come into play.

In other cases where live, face-to-face meetings are not warranted (or not allowed because of COVID-19 or the next crisis,) bridge as much of the gap as possible by using video-conferencing tools and by giving people time and space to explain their feelings and attitudes on phone calls and in digital communication.

May 5

Solving the Post-COVID-19 Marketing Puzzle to Replace Customers Lost Forever

Puzzle pieces Getty

Your customers are never coming back. Yes, the sun will come out. The bans will be lifted. Business will resume. But things will never be the way they were before. Each of us is changed. Our businesses are changed. Given that, there is no chance that your old offerings are going to meet the needs, hopes and desires of your changed customers without changes. Trying to sell your old offerings to the customers you had is a recipe for disaster. Instead, take a marketing, puzzle-solving approach to rebooting your business – creating, delivering, and communicating new offerings.

Those approaching problems with a marketing perspective, start with potential customers' needs, hopes and desires and then figure out ways to create, deliver, and communicate offerings that satisfy those potential customers.

This is different than those approaching problems with a sales perspective, who start with existing offerings and figure out how to find, serve, and satisfy the most appropriate customers for those offerings.

And, this is why the most successful organizations are going to tackle marketing first, then sales as part of rebooting their businesses post COVID-19.

Create new offerings

Relook at your SWOT with fresh, post-COVID eyes. Take a hard look at your internal strengths and weaknesses, being honest with yourself about what you're good at and not so good at. Then scan the new world for opportunities and threats.

The magic in this exercise is much as it always was:

- Crossing internal strengths and external opportunities to yield key leverage points.
- Crossing internal weaknesses and external threats to yield business issues.

What's different is the sudden jump-shift in opportunities and threats. If the new threats have not already put you out of business, shore up your weaknesses to survive. Then turn your attention to the new opportunities. Those will prompt your new offerings.

Dig deep to understand changes in potential customers' needs, hopes and desires. If you've got strengths that allow you to satisfy those, you're off to the races. In the best of all cases, this will involve repositioning your current offerings to do that. Second prize would be modifying your current offerings appropriately. Third prize would be creating entirely new offerings based on your strengths.

In any case, the point is to start by understanding the changes in the world and then figuring out how you can best adapt to those changes.

Deliver those offerings

The world's supply chains broke. All of a sudden, delivery is dramatically harder than anyone ever imagined. So, not only do you have to figure out how to create new offerings for changed customers, you have to figure out how to pull them together and get them to those customers.

The main point here is to make sure you can deliver before you promise to deliver.

- Make sure you have a reliable source for all your inputs.
- Make sure you can produce physical products.
- Make sure you can deliver your products and services – in the way your customers want them delivered. In particular, make sure you've got a way to deliver services virtually. The shift from physical to virtual is never going to swing all the way back.
- Make sure you can provide after-sale services at the appropriate level either physically or virtually.

Communicate your offerings

Once you've created and ensured you can deliver your new offerings, turn your attention to selling. I'm not in any way suggesting selling is bad. It just needs to follow the first two marketing steps.

Every sales funnel there ever was is a variation of AIDA – Awareness, Interest, Desire, Action.

Awareness is the price of entry into the funnel. Can't have a conversation with someone that doesn't know you exist. Start by going broad, investing minimal time and money to reach a wide range of potential prospects.

Interest. Here's where your conversations start. Once you know someone has a problem you can solve, and they are aware of you and your offerings, you can share information to start to figure out if your offerings are best to solve their problems.

Desire. Interest, like objectives, is more general. Desire, like goals, is specific. Desire kicks in when your prospects realize that your offerings are specifically right for them. Your puzzle pieces fit together.

Action. Having made the sale conceptually, close it and deliver.

When You Have to Cut, Cut Decisively

The Powell Doctrine is to avoid war, using all the force necessary to achieve a decisive and successful ongoing result. Earlier, I wrote about applying that to business leadership. Here, let's apply it to cutting back when you're over-extended. Use the same steps, with a slight twist. The main point is to cut deeper than you think you need to so you don't ever have to do it again.

1) Get to the ground truth

Ground truth is unvarnished, unfiltered truth about the harsh reality. Start with the assumption that if things are not going well, things are probably worse than you've been led to believe. When organizations are in trouble, people go into survival mode. And people under stress narrow their focus and make bad decisions.

One tool to help you get at ground truth is range forecasting. Don't tell people that you don't believe their single point forecast for revenues, costs or timing. That just makes them defensive. Instead, ask for their 80% confidence range. A one-million-dollar estimate is different than "somewhere between $800K and a million" and "somewhere between one and two million."

A second tool is a SWOT analysis. Look hard at your real internal strengths and weaknesses. Look at external opportunities and threats. Then:

- Cross internal strengths and external opportunities to get at key leverage points.
- Cross internal weaknesses and external threats to get at business issues.

2) Set a decisive objective

A decisive objective at a decisive place and time is one which, if you gain it, you win - what Clausewitz called the "strategic center of gravity." Retrenchment mode is different than growth mode. As long as you are sinking into mud, you're going to keep going down. What you want is to plant your feet on bedrock and start your new ascent.

The trap is to try to do both at the same time. This is not about preserving the option to grow over the short term. It's about getting to bedrock as fast as possible so you can grow later.

3) Make decisive cuts at decisive places and time

The essence of strategy is the creation and allocation of resources to the right place at the right time over time. Generally, this is about concentrating your efforts to create a decisive competitive advantage versus your competition.

When cutting, you're doing the opposite. Instead of focusing on your leverage points to create a decisive competitive advantage you're trying to eliminate business issues to survive.

Triage your work efforts and people.

1. Group 1 are things that are strong enough and don't need your attention. Leave them alone.
2. Group 2 are things that are in trouble and can be helped. Shore them up.
3. Group 3 are things that are beyond help. Make them go away – completely. Make sure you're cutting the money, the people and the work. If you don't cut the work, someone else has to do it, putting more stress on them. And, people under stress make bad decisions.

4) Prepare your troops for success

You don't owe people lifetime employment. But it is in your best interest to help them succeed. This means helping them learn and develop skills they can apply throughout their careers. This means supporting people on the way out.

- It's the right thing to do.
- What goes around, comes around. You never know when you might run into them again.
- Everything communicates. Those left behind will pay attention to how you treat people on the way out as a sign of what matters to you and how you might treat them when it's their turn.

And you need to help those moving into new roles. This means everybody because everyone's roles are different after decisive cuts. Even if nothing has changed in their official roles, the changes around them mean they have different internal suppliers and customers and likely need to work differently.

Relook at or reconfirm their direction, bounded authority, new resources, and accountability.

5) Be personally present at the point of decision

Deliver as much of the bad news yourself as you can. Utilize the Stockdale Paradox to combat denial –"unwavering faith that you can and will prevail with the discipline to confront the most brutal facts of current reality." The people following you need to see that from you to help them believe in their own future.

May 19

How to Mitigate the Mission-Crippling Risk of An Executive Chair, Operating Partner, Or Over-reaching Boss?

mission-crippling risk Getty

In theory, clarity around decision-rights solves a multitude of working relationship problems. In practice, over-reaching bosses, by definition, are prone to over-reach. Thus, the only way to mitigate the mission-crippling risk of an executive chair, operating partner or over-reaching boss is to build and maintain a two-way trusting relationship over time.

Let's talk about the level of risk, the five-levels of decision rights, and what it takes to build and maintain trust.

Mission-Crippling Risk

As an executive onboarding into a new role, look at organizational risk, role risk and personal risk to come up with an overarching assessment. Our onboarding risk calculator can help you do that and suggests you follow triage guidelines once you've assessed your risk.

- If the risk level is **relatively low**, things should go well if you get a head start; manage your message; set direction and build your team; and then sustain momentum and deliver results over your first 100-days and beyond.
- If there's a **manageable** level of risk, follow the same prescriptions as if the risk level were low while keeping your eyes open for the particular risks of your situation.
- If there are potentially **mission-crippling** issues with this role for you, you will need to address them before you start to reduce your likelihood of failure.
- If the risk is **extreme** or insurmountable, consider walking away or at least having a back-up plan.

The existence of an executive chair or operating partner if you're the CEO, or any over-reaching boss is a mission-crippling issue in its own right. You can't do your job unless your boss trusts you to do your job and lets you do it. It's impossible to build a trusting relationship with the people working with you and for you if your boss is second-guessing your decisions.

Accept that no executive chair, operating partner, or over-reaching boss ever sees themselves as the problem. They think they're helping, guiding and protecting you – sometimes from yourself.

Decision Rights

The clearer you can be about who makes which decisions with whose input, the better will be your working relationship with your boss. Many find this decision-level framework useful:

Level 1 – Boss decides on their own without your input – Things like your compensation and politically sensitive things from which you need to be shielded. (The less of the latter, the better.)

Level 2 – Boss decides with your input. These decisions generally involve the allocation of resources beyond your span of control. For example, if you're the CEO, you'll need your boss or the board's agreement to major strategic changes like mergers and acquisitions and divestitures.

Level 3 – Shared decisions. Nightmare. Avoid as much as possible. Shared decisions across peers require unanimous consent – tough to get. Shared decisions with your boss are really level 2 decisions.

Level 4 – You decide with boss's input. The more of these, the better. You're almost always better off getting your boss's perspective on the way to your decision. Asking for it builds trust.

Level 5 – You decide on your own without boss's input. These are time-sensitive tactical decisions you just need to make. Always a good idea to inform your boss afterwards about these.

Building and Maintaining Trust

Trust is earned over time, not negotiated in advance.

It is in the best interests of your executive chair, operating partner, or boss for you to succeed. If you're one of the 40% of new leaders that fail in their first eighteen months, your board and/or boss will be hurt almost as much as you.

They and their colleagues think part of their job is to help you succeed. They want to be involved in helping you make the right decisions. They want to help manage programs or projects to give you increased leverage. This is why you should start by assuming positive intent on their parts.

And you should remember the best way to build and maintain trust is to be
trustworthy. It is in your best interest to help them help you succeed.

- Clarify decision rights.
- Don't get upset about level 1 decisions.
- Help them make level 2 decisions.
- Invite, welcome and value their input into level 4 decisions.
- Inform them about level 5 decisions.

And be flexible, evolving decision rights as your mutual levels of trust
increase.

May 26

Onboarding into The New Normal Post Covid-19

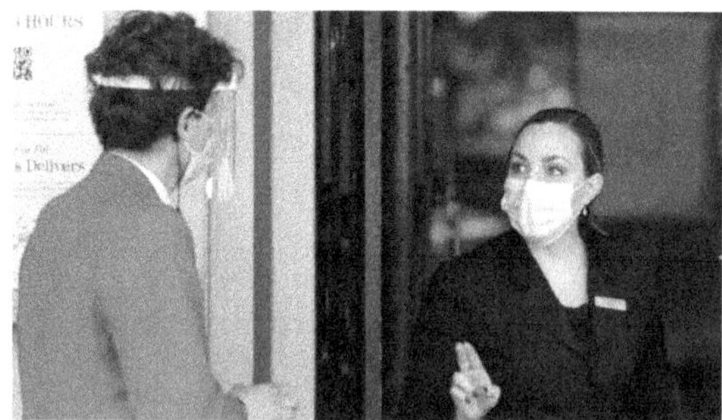

The new normal AFP via Getty Images

Covid-19 will have both temporary and enduring effects. It is both a crisis
to be managed and a cause to hit a restart button to get yourself and your
organization ready for the new normal. How you onboard into a new
organization is one particularly important part of that – and especially how
you connect with people working remotely.

A million years ago, we did a lot of work tracking the evolution of healthy
behavior as part of understanding Puritan Cooking Oil's consumers. We
learned:

- Most people generally increase their propensity for healthy
  behavior and decrease their propensity for unhealthy behavior
  over time – normal evolution.

- Some people experience a health trigger event causing them to adopt a whole bunch of healthy behaviors quickly – point of inflection.
- At some point, people get fed up with all the new healthy behaviors and drop back – point of defection.
- But they drop back to a level higher than they had been tracking to and increase their propensity for healthy behavior from then on at a faster pace than before – new normal.

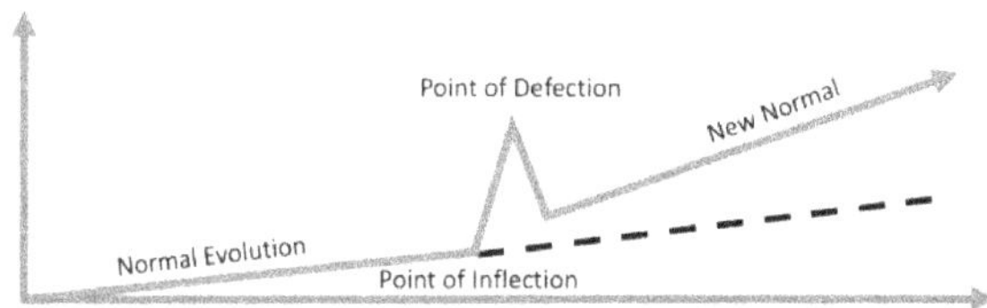

[Some of the health trigger events were obvious and some were surprising. There were positive events like the birth of a child and negative events like medical diagnosis or sudden illnesses for them or others. One of the most impactful events was a 25th high school reunion. People got a save the date for their reunion and immediately said "I'm not showing up looking like this."]

Expect Covid-19 to have a similar impact. We're experiencing a whole bunch of changes right now. When it's over, we'll drop back to a new normal that will be dramatically different than what we had been heading for. This is almost certainly going to be the case with the digital/online shift, and our approaches to health and safety, and risk management and contingency planning.

Digital/Online Shift

The shift to digital and online has been dramatic. By the first week of April, the Commerce Department reported that online U.S. retail sales was higher than general merchandise for the first time ever. Separately, 9% of people polled by CNBC said they worked from home before Covid-19. Now it's 42%. These will never go back to their pre-Covid-19 levels, with huge implications for retail, offices and real estate. Witness Facebook's move to let many employees work from home permanently.

Given that, make sure you're prepared to achieve success in the "Work from home" age. A critical part of getting a head start in a new job is now getting up to speed on your new organization's technology platforms. Make sure you can connect with people working online in the way they are used to connecting.

And then do it.

Get a head start on your new relationships by connecting with people even before you start.

Health and Safety

On the one hand, many of the Covid-19 restrictions are temporary. People will eventually take off their masks, get within six feet of each other and maybe even shake hands. (Though there are certainly some pairs of people that may avoid that forever.) On the other hand, this experience has to change everyone's attitude to health and safety. We all know how fragile things are and how fast they can go bad. Health and safety concerns are going to be much more front of mind in future planning endeavors and ways of working.

Part of this goes to your situation assessment. As you look at customers, collaborators, capabilities, competitors and conditions, make sure to consider the impact of Covid-19 on all of them. And make sure to consider the possible impact of future health and safety concerns and make them part of your own communication.

Risk Management and Contingency Planning

Almost everyone was surprised at how fast the supply chain collapsed and demand evaporated. Too many companies had gone too far down the road of single-source, just-in-time supply or relied on a few customers or a few types of customers. They had no back up or contingency plans. Never again. Going forward all of us are going to pay more attention to risk management and have back-up contingency plans.

Shame on you if you don't have a backup plan for everything. Perhaps the most important lesson we've all learned is to prepare for the unexpected.

How to Set Tactical Leaders Up for Success?

Portugal Plant Opening SOPA Images/LightRocket via Getty Images

Strategies can be theoretically elegant and practically useless without the right tactical leaders. Too many strategic leaders assume if they just set the direction and explain it well enough, everyone will follow them and they will succeed. Wrong. The direction needs to be adjusted tactically on a continual basis – by tactical leaders who need direction, and resources, and bounded authority and accountability.

"Strategy" comes from the Greek word *strategos* – the art of the general – arranging forces before the battle. It's about the utilization of all forces, through large-scale, long-range planning and development, to ensure security or victory.

"Tactics" comes from *taktikos* – the use and deployment of forces in the actual battle in line with strategies.

This is complicated by nested battles. One level's strategies and tactics are the next level's missions and strategies.

Imagine for example,

- The CEO chooses to expand into South America and appoints a President of South America for their business.
- The President of South America chooses to start in Brazil and appoints a Country Manager for Brazil.
- The Brazil Country Manager chooses to build the first manufacturing plant in Portugal and ship product from there to Brazil.

The CEO never imagined building a plant in Portugal.

	CEO	Pres. S. America	Manager, Brazil
Mission (why)	Build business	Build business in South America	Build business in Brazil
Strategy (how)	Expand geographic footprint	One country at a time	Secure reliable source of supply
Tactics (what)	Enter South America	Brazil first	Supply from Portugal

Setting up tactical leaders for success

This is a two-edged sword. A strategic leader engaging in Level Four Delegation has to give tactical leaders the direction, resources and authority they need. The tactical leader has to accept and own accountability:

1. Direction/objectives/desired results/intent
2. Resources (human, financial, technical or operational)
3. Authority to make tactical decisions within strategic boundaries/guidelines
4. Accountability and consequences (standards of performance, time expectations, positive and negative consequences of success and failure)

Let's flesh these out.

Direction/objectives/desired results/intent

One of the classic suggestions for delegation is to delegate the what and not the how. Direction is about the what.

Give people clear direction around where play choices - the hills you want them to take. This is about making the objectives clear. Recall objectives are general things like, strengthen the brand, increase market share, or decrease spending.

Quantify those objectives, turning them into desired results – measurable goals.

And tell people how their objectives fit with others' objectives. Intent is the key to this, linking their output to the next group's tasks. Understanding the strategic leader's intent enables tactical leaders to adjust along the way as they see better tactical ways to achieve that intent.

Resources (human, financial, technical or operational)

Direction is useless without resources. Make sure you're resourcing your most important priorities with the people required for success, the financial investment the need, appropriate technical support, and operational systems and support to make them real.

Authority to make tactical decisions within strategic boundaries/guidelines

This is often the hardest piece for strategic leaders. It's hard for them to let go of tactical decisions. But they have to. If they try to make tactical decisions regarding the use of resources in the middle of implementation, they will inevitably slow things down. These decisions have to be made by the leaders closest to the point of decision.

But not in a vacuum.

Those tactical leaders need authority to make decisions – but it should be bounded authority. Give them a framework for their decisions so they know how to think about them. Give them boundaries so they know how far they can go on their own and when they need to escalate decisions.

If you do that, you can give your tactical leaders the tactical authority they need with confidence that their decisions will fit your strategy.

Accountability and consequences (standards of performance, time expectations, positive and negative consequences of success and failure)

While direction, resources and authority can flow from strategic to tactical leaders, accountability cannot be forced. It's only valuable if tactical leaders understand and own accountability for their tactical decisions. They need to own the standards of performance. They need to commit to time expectations. They need to be willing to accept the positive and negative consequences of their success and failure.

How to Answer the Only Question That Matters as An Executive Onboarding into A New Role on Day One?

What does this mean for me? Getty Images

What does this mean for me? That's the only question anyone has for an executive onboarding into a new role. No one cares about you. All they care about is how you're going to impact their lives. And they're scared. Change is uncertain and unsettling. This is why you have to establish your credibility, connect emotionally, rationally confirm the current reality, and paint an inspirational picture of a shared future.

This is counter-intuitive for most new executives. They think others want to learn about their background, how they like to work, and their vision and values. People do want to understand those – but not first. They can't hear anything until they believe they're going to be safe. And, in a crisis, this is magnified exponentially.

Start with Aristotle's Ethos – Pathos – Logos framework:

Ethos gets at why the audience should listen to you – credibility and character.

Pathos is about connecting with the audience's emotions.

Logos is about convincing with logic or reason.

Add the emotional – rational – inspirational framework:

Emotional: Be authentic, relatable and vulnerable as you empathize with how they are feeling.

Rational: Lay out the hard facts and possible impacts of the current situation.

Inspirational: Paint an optimistic view of the future and how you all can get to that future together.

Mash those together, adding-in the need to converge into an organization before you try to evolve it, and you get these building blocks for your day one communication.

Credibility. Someone needs to give the audience a reason to listen to you - but not you. Let someone else introduce you and explain why you're the right person for this job. They can say things you can't. If they talk about you've done in the past, that helps others believe you are the right leader for this situation. They are endorsing you and making people more willing to listen to you. If you say those things, you're bragging. And no one likes braggarts.

Emotional Connection. The person introducing you should give your audience a reason to listen to you. Follow that by making the audience want to listen to you. Do this by giving them insight into your character. Help them relate to you in a way that makes them think you've been in their shoes or, at least, understand what they're going through. Per above, be authentic, relatable and vulnerable as you empathize with how they are feeling.

Rational Current Reality. Having connected emotionally, now you can look at the hard facts of the current situation. This is the first part of the Stockdale Paradox - realism. This is cold, rational, logical and reasonable. Stay as close to the facts and as far away from opinion as you can. New York Governor Andrew Cuomo has started every one of his daily Covid-19 press conferences with facts. He is being crystal clear on when he is sharing facts and when he is sharing opinions. Do that.

Inspirational Shared Future. End with the second part of the Stockdale Paradox – optimism. Paint a picture of the future in which all can envision themselves. It's not about your vision. It's about their vision. This is where you inspire them and make them want to work with you to get to that better place together. Note that "work with you" is hugely different than "follow you." Giving them the answer on your first day tells them you don't value their input. Share the vision. Build the path together.

If you do this right, your audience will think:

I should listen to this new leader (credibility)

I want to listen to this new leader (emotional connection)

This new leader understands our predicament (rationally)

I like this new leader's direction (inspired)

This has been about day one first impressions. Once you've established your credibility, think in terms of emotional connection – rational assessment – inspirational direction.

Many new leaders go through New Leader Assimilation sessions to answer questions about their background, ways of working, vision and values. This flips the communication from bragging to responding.

A month or so in, pivot from asking questions and converging to evolving by co-creating a shared purpose and imperative. Telling yields compliance. Selling, testing or consulting invites contribution. Co-creation inspires commitment.

June 16

Chance Encounters Have Been Obliterated By COVID-19. Here's How to Replace Them.

Chance encounter over a coffee break Toronto Star via Getty Images

At some level, you know the problem. COVID-19 has switched your world from live to virtual. It turns out there are some nice things about this including savings in commuting and travel time and costs and more efficient meetings. Still, there's something missing – chance encounters and informal conversations. They're important over time and need to be deliberately replaced with excuses to contact and scheduled informal conversations.

The Importance of Chance Encounters

Weber, Magnolfi and Lindsay made the point in 2014 that 'chance encounters and interactions between knowledge workers improve performance." In particular, "three key elements of successful communication:

exploration (interacting with people in many other social groups),

engagement (interacting with people within your social group, in reasonably equal doses), and

energy (interacting with more people overall)."

They cite one company that ripped out its smaller coffee machines and break spaces, replacing them with coffee machines and spaces that could accommodate 120 people each. "In the quarter after the coffee-and-cafeteria switch, sales rose by 20%, or $200 million, quickly justifying the capital investment in the redesign."

COVID-19's Impact

There are two parts to productivity: efficiency and effectiveness. We're finding ways to work more efficiently virtually, but sacrificing the effectiveness of live, person-to-person exploration, engagement and energy. There's an interpersonal connection that happens live and in-person that can never be replicated virtually. And chance encounters don't happen at all virtually.

By definition, chance encounters happen by chance and are unplanned. Smart workspaces are increasingly designed to encourage and enable those chance encounters. But they're not happening with people forced to be physically isolated.

Let's explore two fixes: creating excuses to contact people and scheduling informal conversations.

Excuses to Contact

Instead of waiting to bump into someone by chance virtually – which is never going to happen - find or create an excuse to contact them. In one sense, the excuse doesn't matter. You're trying to replace chance encounters. On the other hand, the more meaningful and helpful the excuse is, the better it will be received. You might, for example, contact people to:

Tell or give them something:

- Remind them about something.
- Thank them for doing something nice for you or others.
- Compliment them on something they did.
- Apologize for something you did.
- Offer words of encouragement.
- Offer counsel.
- Share some information or news.
- Share a new idea.
- Share a link to an article or video they may find useful.
- Forward a quote.

Persuade or ask them about something:

- Volunteer to help them.
- Schedule an informal conversation.
- Ask them to connect you to someone else.

Just test things:

- Check in on them.
- Connect on Twitter or LinkedIn, follow their blog.

Consult with them:

- Ask a question.
- Ask for help.
- Ask their opinion.

Co-create:

- Brainstorm an idea.

That's just a starter list. While you can't bump into people by chance when you're quarantined, you can bump into an excuse to contact others. Be open to those excuses. Leverage them.

Scheduled Informal Conversations

The suggestion here is not to replace formal meetings with informal conversations – though in a lot of cases, that's also a good idea. This is about replacing chance encounters that begin with things like,

"So glad I bumped into you. Been wanting your views on…"

"Do you have a few minutes after our meeting?"

" Let's walk out together…."

"Which way are you heading? I'll detour with you."

Those only happen if you're in the same physical space. If you're not, be proactive. Schedule virtual office hours so people can drop by. Reach out to the people to make the time for conversations.

You don't really need an objective, agenda, or a lot of time.

What you do need is to have conversations that build relationships with people in your social group, in other social groups, and with more people overall.

Schedule the conversations. But don't over-plan them. Let them flow so that you and the people you are conversing with can explore ideas together, interact with each other and feed off each other's energies.

You might, for example, think about the ten most important people you want to have ongoing interactions with them. Each day, find an excuse to contact one of them or have an informal conversation with them. Go through the list one person per day. Then, start over.

How Your Chief of Staff Can Give You Increased Leverage

Andrew Cuomo and Chief of Staff, Melissa DeRosa Getty Images

Your chief of staff can give you increased leverage by managing you, priorities, programs and projects, and communication. Most leaders are unbalanced. They are relatively stronger or weaker across strategy, organization and operations.

- Those relatively weaker operationally need strong chief operating officers.
- Those relatively weaker organizationally need strong chief human resource officers.
- Those relatively weaker strategically need strong chief strategy officers, often titled CFO, CMO, General Counsel or the like.

Those few balanced leaders must have strong chiefs of staff to give them leverage across operational, organizational and strategic processes. At the same time, strong chiefs of staff always give leaders more leverage by managing the leaders themselves, and by managing priorities, programs and projects, and communication.

Manage You

An effective chief of staff (COS) will manage your schedule/diary in line with your priorities so you can spend more time on the most important things and less time on less important things. Part of this is managing distractions - either making them go away or dealing with them with a minimal use of your time – if any. This requires the COS to be your close confidant, understanding your priorities and helping you think things through.

Decision rights matter. Be make sure you and your COS are clear on when they are:

- Making a recommendation or request for you to decide or do something.
- Seeking your contribution/input on a decision or action that they are going to make or do. (COS won't go forward without your input.)
- Informing you about a decision or action they intend to make or do so you are aware, can learn, and can veto or change as appropriate (COS will move forward unless you re-direct them. Silence is consent.)
- Following up for you. This is about influencing others' schedules/diaries in line with your priorities so priority items aren't getting dropped or delayed by others

Manage Priorities, Programs, and Projects

A strong chief of staff acts as your proxy, or program or project manager as appropriate – especially with regard to things that cut across others' areas of responsibility. This is not about doing the work, but assembling resources, coordinating, and working behind the scenes to enable others to do the work. Let's clarify some definitions:

- "Priorities" include ongoing strategic, organizational and operational processes and the one or two critical long-term initiatives you choose to own yourself. In either case, COS gives you resource and coordination leverage.
- "Programs" are the main longer-term components of those priorities, generally tracked and managed monthly.
- "Projects" are the sub-components of programs, generally tracked and managed weekly.
- "Tasks" are the actual work that rolls up into projects, programs and priorities. These are generally tracked and managed at least daily by front-line supervisors.

Manage Communication

An effective chief of staff will bring issues and opportunities to your attention as appropriately gathered in conversations, emails, tweets, blogs, etc. They also help you think through and implement your message and communication efforts.

This is a non-trivial task. Everything communicates - everything you do and say and don't do and don't say and the order in which you say or do it. Your chief of staff has to be able to challenge you and re-direct or sharpen the thinking behind your communication.

Levels of Delegation

1. Do self well
2. Do self well enough
3. Delegate and manage
4. Delegate and not manage
5. Do later
6. Do never

With this in mind, your chief of staff should help you assign levels to things, assist you on level 1 and 2 priorities as much as possible, and own all level 3-6 priorities so you can focus your best thinking on level 1 things.

Meeting Agendas

Your chief of staff should ensure there is an agenda for every meeting or call in which you are involved. While meetings run the gambit from simple to complex, every agenda should include:

- The objective of the meeting.
- Meeting timing and methodology (live, video, audio.)
- What you are being asked to do in the meeting (decide, contribute, learn.)
- Meeting attendees, their role in the meeting by agenda item (decide, contribute, learn,) and anything new you should know about their ability to decide, contribute or learn.
- Pre-reads for you and attendees to digest in advance to help you decide, contribute or learn.

Prime Chief of Staff CEO Catherine Bernardi's take on this is close, but not exactly the same as mine. She told me, "The Chief of Staff is a cross-functional role focused on improving executive effectiveness. Successful Chiefs of Staff understand that improving an organization's effectiveness begins with the effectiveness of the leader themselves. As a strategic "right hand," a Chief of Staff can improve leader effectiveness in six key areas: rationalizing the leader's time; focusing on their priorities; delivering strong results; promoting communication; building on their leader's strengths; and, helping the leader make strong decisions."

The Only Way to Avoid Compound Errors in Business and Life

Avoiding compound errors Getty Images

We all do it. We make a mistake and then, in trying to fix it, make it worse. And we all know the way to stop the cycle: own up to the mistake, accept the new reality, and build from there.

It's almost a cliché.

"Don't consider sunk costs."

"Don't throw good money after bad."

"When you're in a hole, stop digging."

Yet, that's exactly what people do. Companies have cash flow issues. So, they cut staff. That hurts their revenues, leading to more cash flow issues. So, they cut more staff. And they're in a death spiral.

Or they get into trouble with customers and make unrealistic promises to make their customers feel better over the short term. Whether or not it works over the short term, it's not sustainable over the long term.

Golfers hit shots into the woods. Then they try highly unlikely shots right at the green instead of hitting safer shots back onto the fairway first.

That "instead" involves three steps:

1. Own up to the mistake.
2. Accept the new reality.
3. Build from there.

Own up to the mistake

We all make mistakes. We misread things. We miss new information. Sometimes we just guess wrong. But it's rarely the first mistake that's the problem. It's the cover up. Like the old saying suggests, share good news with your boss in good time, but run to your boss with bad news. They can't help you if they don't know.

Alexander Pope put it well a very long time ago, "No one should be ashamed to admit they are wrong, which is but saying, in other words, that they are wiser today than they were yesterday."

Accept the new reality

A mistake creates a new reality. If step one is owning up to the mistake, step two is figuring out the impact of that mistake on the current reality. If the mistake's impact is

- **Insurmountable**, cut your losses and walk away.
- **Mission-crippling,** take the hit, correct or mitigate the impact of the mistake, and hit a restart button.
- **Manageable,** manage the fall-out from the mistake and move on with appropriate adjustments.
- **Minor,** capture the learning, file the mistake away as a data point and move on.

Build from there

A sales team kept just missing each quota each month. Each month they'd meet in the middle of the month to map out how they could make up as much of their shortfall as possible over the remaining weeks. They generally got close, but rarely over the line. One month the sales manager called a halt.

"I don't want to talk about this month anymore. Let's focus on what we can do to get ahead of the curve for next month."

Their final customer calls for the month were different. Instead of begging customers to accelerate orders to help them hit their numbers, they talked about what they could do to help their customers leverage their products to build their customers' businesses over time.

They made the next 26 quotas and became the top district in the country.

Get it?

They'd kept compounding their errors every month. By asking their customers to accelerate purchases at the end of each month, they started the next month in a hole. They were spending their precious time with customers trading deposits in their emotional bank accounts for short-term business.

It didn't stop, couldn't stop, until the sales manager owned up to the mistake of starting each month behind the curve.

He decided the barriers were insurmountable in one month and cut his losses – literally telling his team to give up on achieving their goals that month.

That allowed them to change their approach and build from there by putting their customers' needs first and making deposits into their emotional bank accounts instead of withdrawals.

Implications for you

Stop compounding tactical errors now. Own your mistakes. Reassess your current reality. Shift from a defensive back foot to a forward-looking front foot and build from there.

Root out systemic compound errors. Pay attention to the ABCs of behavioral modification: antecedent, behavior, consequence. Make sure you are prompting and rewarding the right things. And, make sure you are not providing positive reinforcement of undesirable behaviors or negative reinforcement of desirable behaviors leading to systemic compound errors.

Post-Pandemic Re-booting Through Maslow's Needs Hierarchy

Curtain Call Getty Images

COVID-19 has reset everyone's progress up Maslow's hierarchy of physiological, safety, belonging, self-esteem, and self-actualization needs. As you re-boot your relationships with internal and external stakeholders including customers, you're going to have to meet them where they are and move back up the hierarchy together. Remember it's a competitive world. Play not to lose on hygiene physiological and safety factors. Then differentiate to grow market share or share of mind on belonging, self-esteem and self-actualization benefits.

Competitive Positioning

Positioning is the way others think and feel about your offering. Consider:

- Target audience
- Frame of reference
- Benefit
- Support/attributes which in turn includes permission to believe your benefit, and your brand character/attitude/voice

To [Target Audience], your brand is the brand of [Frame of Reference] that best delivers [Benefit] because of [Support/Attributes]

Value Equation

People's perception of "best delivers" is the result of the value equation – whether or not people explicitly go through the calculation.

$$VALUE\ (relative,\ perceived) = f\ \frac{BENEFITS\ (relative,\ perceived)}{COSTS\ (relative,\ perceived)\ (money,\ time,\ stress,\ etc.)}$$

Relative perceived VALUE is a function of relative perceived BENEFITS / relative perceived COSTS

The ultimate benefits are emotional feelings derived from positive features. Costs include money, time, stress, and the like.

One fundamental strategic choice is whether to focus on benefits or costs. Organizations and brands focused on benefits invest in innovation to build and sustain premium prices and positions versus their competition. Those focused on costs strive for efficiency across the board to become and stay the low-cost and low-price provider.

In either case, remember that for you to gain market share or share of mind, someone or something else has to lose market share or share of mind. Expect them not to be happy when that happens. Expect them to change what they're doing to win share back.

This is why you have to keep investing in innovation or cost-cutting to stay ahead of your ever-improving competition.

Hygiene

In the 1950s and 60s, Fredrick Herzberg taught us about job satisfiers and job dissatisfiers.

The dissatisfiers like company policies, supervision, relationships with supervisor and peers, work conditions, salary, status and security are hygiene factors that need to be good enough not to dissatisfy people. But there are severely diminished returns to taking them beyond good enough.

On the other hand, the more the better with satisfiers like achievement, recognition, the work itself, responsibility, advancement and growth.

Maslow Hygiene Factors

In general, the first two levels of Maslow's hierarchy are hygiene factors. People's physiological and safety needs need to be met well enough for them not to be problems.

The top levels are satisfiers. The more self-esteem and self-actualization, the better.

Belonging benefits are caught in the middle. They are higher-level than hygiene factors, but often not satisfiers on their own. People want to belong to a club, tribe, or fan base. But it's only a differentiating benefit if that membership builds their self-esteem or self-actualization.

Re-boot

One of the tricky things for organizations over the next several months is going to be the shift from focusing on Maslowian satisfiers to hygiene. The issue is that people generally move through Maslow's hierarchy sequentially. They can't even think about the next level up until they've satisfied the level below. And the pandemic sent everyone back to thinking about physiological or safety needs. This creates two traps for organizations:

Trap #1 is not meeting people where they are. You can't sell high-end fashion, esteem-building products to people trying to figure out how to pay for their next meal.

Trap #2 is applying higher order satisfier thinking to hygiene factors. The return on investment to be the safest airline just isn't there. Airlines should invest what it takes to be safe enough. Then, invest in differentiating benefits like experience.

Implications for you

1. **Take a hard re-look at your target audience** and where they are playing on Maslow's hierarchy now. Unless you're providing super high-end products or services, expect your target to have dropped back to concerns about safety or physiological needs.

2. **Meet your target where they are now.** In most cases, this will
    mean focusing on and communicating your physiological and
    safety standards first. But remember that you're playing not to lose
    here. Make your physiological and safety offerings good enough
    and no better.
3. **Then play to win**, investing in and communicating belonging,
    self-esteem or self-actualization benefits to differentiate your
    offering from all others.

July 7

The Difference Between Deputies and Chiefs of Staff

Sheryl Sandberg – Facebook COO (Deputy CEO)

Deputies are second in command empowered to act in their superiors'
absence. Chiefs of staff give their leaders increased leverage by managing
them, priorities, programs and projects, and communication. Each is
important in their own right. Not all leaders fill either or both positions.
Don't be fooled by titles as those acting as deputies or chiefs of staff may
have a very different title. And few people with the title "Vice President"
are actually deputies – including the Vice President of the United States.

Chiefs of Staff

An earlier article on How Your Chief of Staff Can Give You Increased
Leverage went into a detail on how chiefs of staff can manage you,
priorities, programs and projects and communication. The main points are
that chiefs of staff gives you leverage by:

- Managing you, your schedule/diary in line with priorities to minimize distractions.
- Managing priorities, programs and projects as your proxy or program or project managers. This is about assembling resources, coordinating, and working behind the scenes to enable others.
- Managing communication by bringing issues and opportunities to your attention and helping you think through and implement your message and communication efforts.

Essentially, Chiefs of Staff have no positional power. All their authority derives from their superiors.

Deputies

The key to deputies' effectiveness is clarity on how they are empowered to act in their superiors' absence, generally one of these:

1. Speak for the leader at all times in all areas.
2. Ongoing decision-making authority in discrete areas.
3. Temporary decision-making authority in discrete areas.
4. No decision-making authority unless leader is formally incapacitated, dies, resigns, or is removed from office.

Speak for the leader at all times in all areas (Level 1)

Some leaders and their deputies actually are or act as partners. For whatever reason, they may not have chosen to be co-CEOs or co-Presidents. So, one is the official leader and the other is the official deputy. But all their debates and discussions happen behind closed doors. In public, they speak with one voice and it doesn't matter which of them is formally giving approval to anything.

Let's spend a minute on those behind-the-scenes discussions. The most effective deputies are also some of their leaders' most trusted confidants. They bring broad perspectives to discussions with leaders and intimate knowledge of their leaders' context, hopes, needs and priorities. They help leaders sharpen their thinking by challenging it. This can be true whatever the deputies' formal decision-making authority.

Ongoing decision-making authority in discrete areas (Level 2)

Some Chief Operating Officers are effectively deputy-CEOs. We had this at Coca-Cola with Roberto Goizueta as CEO and Doug Ivester as President and Chief Operating Officer. Goizueta was "Mr. Outside," focusing his time on managing the board, outside stakeholders and enterprise strategy. Ivester was "Mr. Inside," managing day-to-day operations. Facebook has the same set up with Sheryl Sandberg essentially acting as Mark Zuckerberg's Deputy CEO.

This is exactly in line with the military concept of an XO or Executive Officer, managing tactical, day-to-day activities so the Commanding Officer can focus on strategy – the deployment of forces before the battle.

Temporary decision-making authority in discrete areas (Level 3)

On the surface, this looks like the way Chiefs of Staff might manage priorities, programs or projects. The difference is that Chiefs of Staff have no positional authority. They must act in their superior's name and refer everything back to that superior for decisions. Deputies have positional authority and can make decisions to move priorities, programs or projects ahead. In RACI terms, while a Chief of Staff or Deputy may be accountable, Deputies will have approving authority as well.

No decision-making authority (Level 4)

The Vice President of the United States has no formal power other than presiding over the senate. Some vice presidents have been asked to manage discrete areas, but they acted more like accountable project managers than approving authorities. As such, the Vice President of the United States is a model of what a leader-in-waiting looks like. They're there in case they're needed.

Other organizations use deputy roles as learning and development opportunities. Deputies shadow leaders so they can see what they do on the way to doing it themselves. It's valuable and, by definition, temporary.

There are many options. Just be clear which you're deploying.

Why The 90/10 Loser Gets the Job Over the 60/40 Winner

Tending toward the mean BLOOMBERG NEWS

If you're looking for a job, strive to be the 90/10 loser instead of the 60/40 winner. It's better to come in first 10% of the time than second 60% of the time.

Candidates for jobs need to convince hiring managers that they can do the job (strengths,) will love the job (motivation,) and will be tolerable (fit) better and more than any other candidate.

This is where the 90/10 versus 60/40 positioning comes into play. To become a 60/40 winner, you have to tend toward the mean so you appeal widely. Those tending toward the mean, round their edges so they offend less people. These people tend to be more acceptable to others (60%) but have less people passionate about them. As a result, they make the cut to be final candidates for jobs more frequently than others, but often come in second place.

90/10 losers don't have that problem. They get rejected out of hand 90% of the time. But the 10% that want them, really want them.

The difference is focus and the courage to talk about what's most important and walk away from opportunities where the fit is less clear.

For example, imagine a hiring manager that says they need someone with strategic, organizational, and operating strengths.

60% of presented candidates come in with solid examples of their strengths in each area. They move on to the next round.

Not you. You come in and explain that you're particularly strong in any one of the three areas and relatively weaker in the other two. Note you're not saying you're weak. You're not saying you're weaker than others. You're just saying you're unbalanced and stronger in some areas than others.

What this does is make the hiring manager think about what they really care about. If they really do want all three areas, you're out. Fine. If they really care about one of the two areas in which you're relatively weaker, you're out. Fine. But if what they really care about is the area in which you are particularly strong, you're now the candidate to beat.

The prescription is to figure out what they should really care about. If it's not your core strength, walk away. If it is your core strength, focus your conversations on that. Talk about that. Of course, there are other things you can do. You'll do them and over-deliver on expectations when the time is right. Then there are things you won't do. You most definitely do not want a job that requires you doing them.

This works after you've got the job as well.

Talk about the things you're most interested in. Learn about them. Practice them. Volunteer for assignments that give you experience in those areas. Build a deep expertise in these things. Guide your own career into these areas directly and indirectly.

Along the way, there are a whole range of other things your employers or clients will ask you to do. Do them. Do them really well. Over-deliver. You'll learn by doing and get better and better. You'll develop strengths in some of these areas. You can deploy those strengths over time. Just don't talk about them.

And there are things you won't do. The key here is to be upfront about those so no one ever asks you to do them. Some of these violate some of your underlying values. Most of them are distractions from what you think are most important. Any moment you spend on somethings less important is a moment you're not spending on what is important. That is the opposite of focus.

Oh, by the way, if you've got someone working for you doing things outside of their core areas of interest, you should do what you need to do to get their focus back on what they care about most. Doing that is a sign of respect. If you don't do that, eventually you'll lose them. They'll burn out or quit. Just because they are doing what you need them to do – and doing it well, does not necessarily mean they're doing what they want to do.

Sometimes you don't want to stand out. Sometimes you do want to tend to the mean. But not when it comes to positioning yourself and your career. Be known for something. Invest in it. Get better at it. Build your expertise. Claim your expertise. Talk about it. And don't talk about the rest.

July 21

40 Tips to Mitigate the 40% Executive Onboarding Failure Rate

Poor fit is the #1 risk. Getty

Most of executive onboarding is just common sense. Still, different people latch on to different nuggets that help their own chances of success in a world in which 40% of new leaders fail in their first 18-months. These 40 tips all nest under the importance of **converging and then evolving** by I) Getting a head start, II) Managing the message, III) Setting direction and building the team and IV) Sustaining momentum and delivering results.

1. **Fit in.** The mismatch between personal preferences and cultural behaviors, relationships, attitudes, values, and environment is the #1 risk and #1 cause of failure.

2. **Deliver.** Failure to deliver is the #2 cause of failure. Sooner, rather than later, get done what they need you to get done.

3. **Adjust.** Obviously, a big part of converging upfront is adjusting to the culture. But adjusting never ends. Keep your eyes open and adjust to changes down the road from anemic to pandemic.

GET A HEAD START

4. **Think through** a five-step career plan including

   1. Your likes and dislikes.
   2. Long-term goals.
   3. Ideal job criteria.
   4. Create options.
   5. Choose the right option given your long-term goal sand ideal job criteria.
   6. Do a gut check.

5. **Adopt a** 90/10 positioning. 60/40 winners tend to the mean and come in 2nd place 6 out of 10 times. 90/10 losers get ruled out immediately 90% of the time and get the job 10% of the time.

6. **Differentiate between what you talk about, will do, and will not do.** Make the piece you talk about as focused as possible. At the same time, know that just because you don't talk about some things doesn't mean you won't do them. But, be clear on what you won't do.

7. **Avoid the** consultant's roller coaster, selling, selling, selling until you reach capacity, then putting all your time and attention into delivering the work you've sold, leaving no time for selling, so that when the work is

done, you have no pipeline. Instead, always keep 20% of your time focused on business development.

Some executives in transition do some consulting work to generate income and keep their skills current. It's a good idea – unless it's taking all your time and keeping you from working your job search. Keep 20% of your time free for your job search.

8. Know there are only three interview questions **– ever.**

1. Can you do the job? (Strengths)
2. Will you love the job? (Motivation)
3. Can we tolerate working with you? (Fit)

9. No one cares about you. They care about what you can do for them.

10. Prepare answers to the only three interview questions **- from their perspective.**

1. Strengths that they need
2. Motivation to do their job
3. Fit with their culture.

11. Avoid the 100-Day Plan for interviews **trap.** If asked to prepare a 100-Day Plan for a final interview, remember it's not about you. Position your plan in the context of their overall objectives and 12-month goals. This leads to what your team needs to get done and then and only then, your 100-Day Plan.

12. Virtual tip **#1: Think classical, not jazz.** Live meetings can have jazz-like flexible agendas. Virtual meetings need deliberate and detailed content, meeting flow, and technology planning, preparation and rehearsals – like a classical orchestra.

Note these tips apply to all virtual meetings including interviews, pre-start conversations, workshops, and the like.

13. Virtual tip #2: Flip the classroom. Send people pre-reads ahead of virtual meetings so you can focus on discussions during those meetings.

14. Virtual tip #3: Keep breakouts to 3-4 people. The perfect size for a live team meeting is 7 people +/- 2. Less than 5 and you risk not having

the full range of diverse perspectives. More than 9 and people are fighting
for air time. But with virtual meetings it's hard to have a real conversation
with more than four people on at a time.

15. Interviews are about selling. Everything is part of the interview.
Every interaction with anyone. Every question. Everything you say and do
should communicate the strengths, motivation and fit they're looking for.
You can't turn down a job offer you don't have. So, sell before you buy.

16. Then do your due diligence. If you paid attention to tip #15 and
focused 100% on selling, you have to do a real due diligence after you've
been offered and before you accept the job.

17. Answer three due diligence questions:

1. What is the organization's sustainable competitive advantage?
   (Organizational risk.)
2. Did anyone have concerns about this role; and, if so, what was
   done to mitigate them? (Role risk)
3. What, specifically, about me, led the organization to offer me the
   job? (Personal risk.)

18. Dig into the culture. The BRAVE framework can help. Make sure
you understand:

- **Behaviors:** Flexible vs. stable discipline | Interdependent vs.
  independent | Enjoyment vs. order
- **Relationships:** Purpose vs. authority | Informal vs. formal
  communications | Diffused vs. hierarchical decisions
- **Attitudes:** Innovation vs. minimum viable strategy | Proactive vs.
  responsive | Learning vs. safety
- **Values:** Purpose as intended vs .as written | Open/shared vs.
  directed learning | Caring vs. results focus
- **Environment:** Open vs. closed layout | Casual vs. formal décor |
  Work-life balance vs. work-focused facilities

19. <u>Assess the overall onboarding risk</u>.

- If it's **low**, do nothing out of the ordinary. (But keep your eyes open for the inevitable changes.)
- If it's **manageable**, manage it in the normal course of events.
- If it's **mission-crippling**, resolve or mitigate before accepting the role.
- If the barriers are **insurmountable**, walk away.

20. Leverage the <u>Fuzzy Front End</u> between accepting and starting a job to

1. Map your stakeholders.
2. Develop a personal 100-Day Action Plan.
3. Get set up.
4. Jump-start learning.
5. Get aligned with your "up" stakeholders and jump-start your key relationships.

For many of you, leveraging the Fuzzy Front End is an important, new idea. Jump-starting relationships not only builds personal bonds but is a key contributor to developing your organizing concept in a way that is impactful and resonates per tip #30.

21. Figure out your <u>onboarding approach</u>: assimilating, converging and evolving fast or slow, or shocking the system based on the organization's need to change, willingness to change, and your risk profile.

22. Get help figuring out <u>which side of the road</u> **to drive on** as every organization drives on different sides of the road in all sorts of different ways which are not going to be intuitively obvious to you. Leverage scouts (who went before,) seconds (committed to helping you,) and spies (helping you behind the scenes.)

23. In a <u>hot landing</u>**,** like all landings in a pandemic,

1. Jump right in to help
2. Learn with everyone else
3. Let your leadership emerge over time.

MANAGE THE MESSAGE

24. Identify the <u>contributors, watchers, and detractors</u>. Contributors share your agenda. Detractors want to stop you. Watchers haven't decided yet.

25. Move them one step at a time. You're not going to turn the detractors into contributors. Instead, turn the contributors into champions, the watchers into contributors, and get the detractors out of the way.

26. <u>Be. Do. Say.</u> No one will believe what you say. They will believe what you do. But if your actions match your words and not your fundamental, underlying beliefs, you will get caught. This is why you have to start there.

27. MAP your communication efforts across Message, Amplifiers, Perseverance. Turn the "old guard" into allies and amplifiers by 1) switching the "we" immediately, never talking about your old company again, 2) standing on the shoulders of giants (the old guard) as you go forward, and 3) leveraging new external platforms for change to enroll the old guard as partners.

28. Do not start by talking about yourself. No one cares about you. Their only question is "<u>What does this mean for me</u>?" In particular, this means do not come in with a presentation about yourself, your values and your ideas.

29. Do start by answering their questions. (Knowing the only question that matters per tip #28.)

30. Clarify your <u>organizing concept</u>. This is the strategy or concept behind your communication points. Get that right so you can flex on the rest.

31. Make your communication <u>emotional, rational and inspirational</u> – **in that order.** Emotionally connect with people first. Then lay out the brutal, rational facts of the situation. Then inspire them to be part of the solution with a specific call to action inspiring new emotions.

SET DIRECTION. BUILD THE TEAM.

32. Co-create a <u>burning imperative</u>. This is the pivot from converging to evolving.

- If you tell people to do something, the best you can ever get is compliance.
- If you want their contribution, sell, test or consult.
- If you want their <u>commitment, you need to co-create.</u>

33. Put in place a <u>milestone management</u> **system.** Strategies are theoretically elegant and practically useless until turned into actions with clarity around what's getting done by when by whom. Make sure someone owns the process and follows through on milestone tracking on a regular basis.

34. Over-invest to accelerate the delivery of one or more projects as <u>early wins</u> to give the team confidence in themselves.

35. Get the <u>right people in the right roles</u> **early on.** The #1 regret experienced leaders have looking back on their careers is not moving fast enough on people.

- **Invest** in under-performing people in the right role.
- **Support** effective people in the right role.
- **Cherish** outstanding people in the right role.
- **Move out** under-performing people in the wrong role.
- **Move over** effective people in the wrong role.
- **Move up** outstanding people in the wrong role.

SUSTAIN MOMENTUM. DELIVER RESULTS.

36. <u>Evolve people, plans and practices</u> **over time.**

37. Systematize a <u>management cadence</u>

- Manage core talent, strategic, capability and operating processes annually/quarterly.
- Track programs monthly.
- Track projects weekly.
- Track tasks daily – perhaps with huddles.

38. Take a <u>strategic approach to risk management</u>: Observe. Assess. Plan. Act.

- **Downplay** minor and temporary changes. Control and stay focused on priorities.
- **Evolve** through minor and enduring changes, factoring into ongoing team evolution.
- **Manage** major and temporary changes. Deploy your incident management response plan.
- **Restart** following a major and enduring change. Jump-shifting your strategy, organization and operations to lead through the point of inflection.

39. <u>Lead through crises</u>

- Think Stockdale Paradox confronting the brutal facts head on with optimism about the future.
- Keep all eyes on your purpose (mission, vision, values/guiding principles)
- Act by i) assessing the situation and scenarios, ii) confirming objectives and intent, iii) laying out options and expected outcomes, iv) prioritizing with accountabilities, v) executing, monitoring, iterating.
- Communicate emotionally, rationally, inspirationally.

40. Keep going. Keep growing, conducting a self-assessment and getting stakeholder feedback to inform course corrections in culture, priorities and leadership approach.

Why Your Cultural Evolution and Survival Depends on Your Middle Managers' Attitude

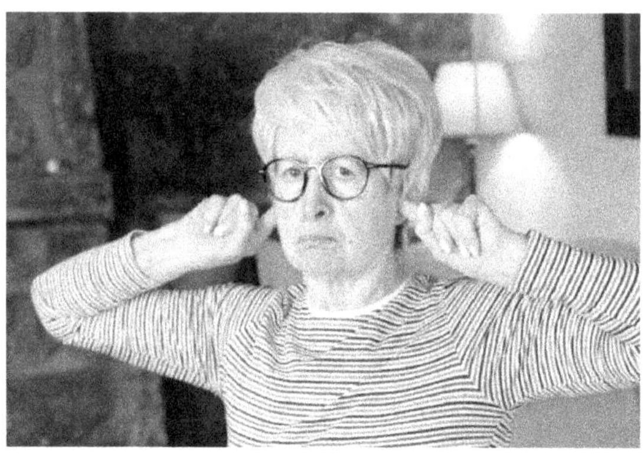

Passive aggressive Getty

So far, your organization has stepped up or faltered in the face of COVID-19 based on your existing cultural responsiveness to change. Going forward, survival will depend on your ability to evolve your culture itself, attitude in particular, and especially the attitude or mindset of middle managers. Those intermediaries can be helpful, neutral or passive-aggressive blockers.

Culture is, at the same time, the only truly sustainable competitive advantage and the weight that's going to bring you down if it doesn't evolve. Per Darwin. "It is not the strongest of the species that survives, nor the most intelligent, but the one most responsive to change."

Let's focus on the middle.

Attitude

Our framework for thinking about culture is BRAVE: Behaviors, Relationships, Attitudes, Values and Environment. The middle dimension is Attitude - one's mental position, feeling or emotion toward a fact or state per Webster. It's a choice. More than that, it's a learned, programmed choice. And it doesn't always match what the CEO thinks is the attitude.

Middle Managers

That's because the choices that matter in this case are the choices made by middle managers.

Again, per Webster, Middle Managers are "management personnel intermediate between operational supervisors and policy-making administrators."

- Senior Executives like the CEO, C-Suite, and enterprise leaders set enterprise-level policies.
- Functional and Business Administrators like department and business unit heads set functional and unit-level policies.
- Middle Managers intermediate between them and
- Operational Supervisors directly supervise operations.
- Operators actually do the work.

Here's the thing about intermediaries, interpreters and translators. They can be extremely helpful. They can be neutral. Or they can block things without you even knowing.

Intermediaries and the like acting neutrally simply pass on your communication, direction, etc. without any changes or comments. It gets through as you sent it.

At their most helpful, intermediaries, interpreters and translators modify or supplement your communication and direction to make it easier for their audience to understand, believe and act in the way you need them to act. This is an art born out of knowing what really matters to policy-making administrators and operational people and finding the overlap between the two.

Blocking often looks like passive aggression. Intermediaries and the like may forget to pass on messages. They may delay messages until the right time. They may modify messages saying their particular geography or units are "different."

They may think they are protecting operators from out of touch policy makers. They make think they are protecting policy makers from irrelevant details. They may be doing it with the wrong intentions. But it's more likely that they think their actions are actually best for the organization as a whole.

Policies, Guidelines and Mindset

In an earlier article, we explored how to balance policies and guidelines to prompt different levels of employee engagement. Let's stick with the definitions of policies and guidelines from that article:

1. **POLICY:** A mandatory, definite course or method of action that all must follow.
2. **GUIDELINE:** A preferred course or method of action that all should generally follow.
3. That article called out the third approach a principle. Instead, let's bring in attitude.
4. **ATTITUDE:** One's mental position, feeling or emotion toward a fact or state.
5. If your middle managers don't agree with a policy, they will comply – as much as they have to. They'll block. They'll go passive aggressive. They'll do the minimum they can get away with. And everyone working with them will know how they feel.
6. If your middle managers don't agree with a guideline, they'll ignore it as something others should generally follow and their teams should specifically ignore.
7. Not agreeing is a "mental position, feeling or emotion toward a fact or state." That's why any successful cultural evolution has to start by helping middle managers evolve their attitudes.

Attitude Evolution

1. **Co-create your aspirational future culture.** Telling yields compliance. Selling, Testing or Consulting is inviting contribution. If you want commitment, co-create – with your policy administrators AND middle managers.
2. **Assess your current culture.** Together, agree where you are.
3. **Identify the few most important dimensions to change first –** most likely starting with one dimension of attitude.
4. **Delegate the work to middle managers.** Give them clear direction, the resources they need, bounded authority and accountability.
5. **Follow through to support their efforts.** Having delegated the work, your role changes. Do your new job. Not theirs.

Leveraging Excuses to Contact to Make Up for Lost Chance Encounters

Let Coca-Cola bring you together LightRocket via Getty Images

It's turning out that, for at least some, working at home is not so bad. Many have found ways to adapt. Some even think they're being more productive. One of the things that's not happening is unplanned chance encounters in hallways, breakrooms, and the like. This has to impact the quality of relationships over time. We all need to compensate for this by paying attention to individuals' personal circumstances when we do interact with them and by leveraging excuses to contact people outside of formal, planned interactions.

Advertising executive Bill Backer's flight to London in January, 1971 was diverted to Shannon, Ireland and held there. After a while, someone took pity on the stranded passengers and wheeled a cooler of Coca-Cola into the waiting room. It brought people together as they gathered around the cooler to share Cokes and their stories. That incident was the inspiration for Backer's song and commercial, "I'd like to teach the world to sing."

It happens in every workplace all over the world. Steve Jobs went so far as to put all the toilets in the middle of his new Apple headquarters so people had to interact with others from different parts of the company.

Productivity of working at home

Productivity is about delivering results. You can be more productive if you deliver the same result with less time or resources – more efficient. Or you can be more productive if you deliver better results with the same time or resources – more effective.

Most of the people that are being more productive working from home are being more efficient. For one, they're saving all sorts of commuting time. Many are finding they get interrupted by work colleagues less often and there are less unplanned meetings. (Of course, some have more unplanned meetings with the other occupants of their quarantine space.)

Partly as a result of this, many are able to concentrate better on things they are working on by themselves. So, for some, there's an effectiveness boost as well.

The same is not going to be true for working with others. Relationships and trust are built over time by working together, caring about each other, and making and fulfilling commitments. There are no way relationships can stay as strong if people are separated by distance. The longer the separation, the more people have to work to maintain those relationships – and their productivity together.

Planned and Unplanned Interaction Time

Somehow there seems to be a little more time for casual conversation in and around meetings in the office. People don't all show up at the same time. Some linger after the close of the meeting. There are often breaks in the middle of the meeting during which people can share a Coke (or coffee or tea or anything else.)

This happens less in conference calls or video calls. People show up closer to the right time (which is a good thing.) They log off at the end of meetings. And they take breaks on their own. Thus, you need to be deliberate about relationship building.

Over time, we should expect virtual and online interactions to get better and better. As they do, the need for excuses to contact may go down. Still, let me suggest some possible ways to do this until the technology catches up.

- **News tips.** Send people links to news tips – perhaps with your point of view.
- **Others' articles.** Send people links to articles you like and then follow up to have a conversation with the people you send them to.
- **Birthdays.** Call or video on their birthdays.
- **Connecting software** like Mandalay or H360 (in which I'm an investor.) These will tell you who else in your organization are working on the same things you are so you can connect with them.
- **Virtual hallways.** Agree to wander through the same video chat room or Zoom meeting room or the like at the same time – just to connect.
- **Virtual team rooms.** Leverage shared documents so people can wander in and out at will and leave thoughts, comments and ideas. Ideally, you'd have three boards in your virtual team room:
  - **Action**: milestones (action, date, accountable, status/help needed,) communication (who, what, when,) parking lot.
  - **Plan**: mission, vision, objectives, goals, strategies, guiding principles
  - **Insights**: customers, collaborators, capabilities, competitors, conditions.

August 4

How to Accelerate Through The COVID-19 Point of Inflection

New ways of working Getty Images

Andy Grove defined a point of inflection as "an event that changes the way we think and act." Given COVID-19's impact, the only question is whether you're going to lead with systemic changes in your organization, market, or industry, or follow others. As McKinsey laid out in their recent article on The Great Acceleration, "Companies that move early in a crisis to get a jump on competitors often maintain that lead for years to come." So, lead by re-looking at your strategy, organization and operations and making appropriate changes all together, in sync, all at the same time.

Three premises:

1. **COVID-19 is one of the defining moments of our time**. Getting your transition right and avoiding avoidable mistakes will accelerate your organization and personal impact, effect, and trajectory. If you're not looking at this as a point of inflection, someone else somewhere else will inflect things for you. And you may not like how that story ends.
2. **Leading is different than managing**. Where managers organize, coordinate and tell, leaders inspire, enable, and co-create. Be an other-focused leader, inspiring and enabling others to do their absolute best together to lead through this "great acceleration" and realize a meaningful and rewarding shared purpose.
3. **Leading requires choices** - and bold, decisive choices at points of inflection. Picking one over-arching strategy, aligned with one culture, organization, and way of operating seems riskier than keeping options open. But choosing to be best in class at one thing versus good enough at many can be the difference between success and failure. Pick one.

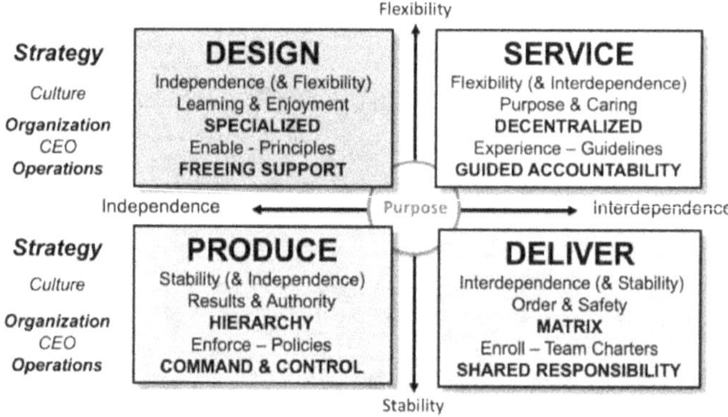

Summary chart from our book, "Point of Inflection"

Do this by working through the enduring impact of the environmental changes, re-committing to your values, and changing your attitude to inform your relational and behavioral choices.

1 *Environment:* Clarify Your Situation and Field of Play

Most freeze in times of uncertainty. They defer choices until things sort themselves out. As McKinsey pointed out, these organizations are going to find themselves following the leader for years to come.

Instead, lay out possible scenarios and options to deal with the different scenarios. It doesn't matter if the scenarios are right. What matters is leveraging them to unfreeze your organization's thinking. In general, you'll want a base case most likely scenario, an optimistic scenario, and a pessimistic scenario.

Then assess the impact of your options under the different scenarios. Choose where to play and how to win while preserving your ability to adjust along the way.

2 *Values:* Align All Around the Organization's Mission, Vision, and Guiding Principles

Your mission (why) probably won't change.

However, this is a great opportunity to relook at your ambition and picture of success – your vision (what.)

Your guiding principles are the things you will not compromise on the way to delivering that mission and achieving that vision – values in action (how.) This is trickier. Your values probably should not change, but your change in vision may dictate a change or evolution in your guiding principles.

3 *Attitude:* Make Choices Around Overarching Strategy, Priorities, and Culture

This is your COVID-19 pivot point. Hopefully you're already aligned around one single overarching strategy to drive how you're going to win (design – produce – deliver – service.)

What changes with COVID-19 should be your resource choice priorities. Move resources from areas in which good enough is good enough into the one most important area in which you choose to be best in class as a top priority and then also to areas in which you choose to be world class.

And make sure your culture evolves in sync with those changes (<u>in</u>dependent – stable – <u>inter</u>dependent – flexible.)

4 *Relationships*: The Heart of Leadership

The change in your resource choice priorities dictates a change in your organization. Do some future capability planning to determine the organization you're going to need to accelerate. Then adjust your ADEPT components: how you acquire, develop, encourage, plan and transition talent on the way to that future state.

Throughout, know that everyone is scared. <u>Connect with them emotionally</u>. Lay out the rational hard facts of the situation. Then inspire the way forward.

5 *Behaviors*: Getting Things Done

Having done all that, follow through to ensure excellent execution focused on what creates the most value for all your stakeholders, leading with a bias to freeing support, command and control, shared responsibilities, or guided accountability as appropriate.

What You Must Learn from Jim Hackett's Failure as Ford's CEO

Jim Hackett AFP via Getty Images

Jim Hackett's exit as Ford's CEO should surprise no one. Billions of dollars in losses, a 40% drop in stock price, and complete lack of clarity around the way forward inevitably had to lead to new CEO. The main lesson from Hackett's case is that while everyone has to converge into an organization before trying to evolve it, you have to time that pivot differently in different circumstances. Hackett moved way too slowly, failed to clarify a coherent strategy or culture and paralyzed the organization.

I've written about Jim Hackett twice before. Once I was right. Once I was wrong.

In writing about his views on How Office Layout Impacts Corporate Culture, I was impressed with Hackett's understanding of the general shift from command and control hierarchies to more collaborative work and how office spaces could enable that.

In writing about Hackett's New Leader's 100-Day Action Plan when he joined Ford in 2017, I said "The bet is that Hackett will succeed. He's got the strengths. He's got the temperament. He's got a strong 100-Day Action Plan. Expect him and Ford to be successful over time." But he failed to be decisive. Ford is fundamentally a design and engineering led manufacturing company. It was in trouble. It needed clear direction from the top – which he failed to give them.

Phoebe Wall Howard's February 13, 2019 article on Hackett in the Detroit Free Press laid out then all the reasons Hackett is on the way out now. Perhaps there was still time then to fix the issue. In any case, Hackett either didn't adjust or didn't adjust fast enough. She suggested:

- **Hackett failed to clarify a coherent strategy.** Ford's then summary of Hackett's vision was too broad and all-encompassing to guide choices. He wanted to "focus on big societal needs," compete for a share of the transportation pool, "create for people what they may not know they need, but will not want to live without," design intelligent, connected vehicles, while "exiting or restructuring weak product lines and markets," and reducing capital expenses all at the same time.
- **Hackett failed either to adapt to the organization's culture or shift it decisively.** His people described him as "not from this world." It's true. He grew up at Procter & Gamble and then Steelcase Office Furniture. He was not from the rough and tumble command and control world of heavy-duty manufacturing.
- **Hackett paralyzed the organization** by promising a restructure and then meting it out like a water-drip torture creating "'paralyzing' tensions waiting for job cuts and strategic decisions.

Implications for you

1) **Deliberately and decisively think through, time, and implement your pivot.** Sometimes you'll want to converge and evolve slowly, sometimes fast. And sometimes (like in a turn-around,) you'll need to shock the organization. Figure it out. Work it. Get on with it.

2) **Make a clear over-arching strategy choice** and align your culture, organization and operations around that choice. Once you figure out if you are fundamentally a design, production, distribution or service organization, everything else flows from that as you work through strategic point of inflection.

3) **Enable the organization with clarity around which decisions are yours, shared or delegated.**

- If the decision is yours to make, get input, think it through, make the decision and move on. Don't pretend it's a shared decision. Don't over-involve people. Don't re-think it unless there's new information. According to Ron Chernow, George Washington got to be particularly good at this by the time he became President, getting input, deciding, and moving on with confidence.

- If the decision is shared, share it. Let people debate and discuss. If you've got ideas, put them on the table as your Best Current Thinking, so people know they can build on them without offending you in any way. Drive to consensus if at all possible – so long as the shared decisions nest within the decisions that you've already made.
- If the decision is delegated, delegate it with confidence. Your job is to support those delegated decisions – just so long as they nest within the shared guidelines.

One leader has 90/6/4 framework. He says 90% of decisions are delegated. His job is to support those. 6% are shared. 4% are his to make – and he expects everyone to support his decisions as he supports the 90% of decisions they make.

August 11

Why Vice President Is Not A Real Job

Joe Biden and Kamala Harris Getty Images

Vice President is not a job. It's a title or level. In the case of the Vice President of the United States, the Constitution defines only two responsibilities: 1) Replace the President in case of death, resignation or inability to discharge the powers and duties of the office, and 2) Preside over the Senate and cast tie-breaking votes. Other Vice Presidents have different jobs. So, the critical question is "Vice President of what?"

Lyndon Johnson and Dick Cheney epitomize opposite ends of the job. President Kennedy put Johnson as VP to get him away from being Senate majority leader and to help him carry Texas in the election. He and his closest advisors wanted as little to do with Johnson as possible and gave him virtually no responsibilities.

At the other extreme, Dick Cheney was as close to a co-president as we've seen. He was the behind-the-scenes leader of the US war on terrorism and one of the main proponents of the US invasion of Iraq, the expansion of wire-tapping by the NSA and other US policy changes.

As Vice President himself, Joe Biden's influence went well beyond his job description. He became one of Barak Obama's closest advisors. He played the role well, often pushing a point of view different than Obama's behind closed doors and then always supporting Obama's ultimate choices in public.

As Biden thought through his own VP choice, that history has to have come into play. His first question was not who, but what. He must have thought through and debated with his advisors what he wanted the VP's role to be before he chose the VP herself. Of course, there was some iteration as different potential VPs had different strengths. He would have adjusted his view of the role to fit the different VPs and the job will evolve as the ultimate VP learns and grows.

Other Vice Presidents

The United States has only one Vice President. Other organizations have more. Some banks have more Vice Presidents than they have customers. In some organizations Vice Presidents report to Directors. In other organizations Directors report to Vice Presidents. So, not only is the job not defined, neither is the level universally clear.

What matters is the role, its authority, accountabilities and responsibilities. Get those agreed and aligned first. Then worry about titles.

Role

Why. Start with why the position exists – their mission. This should
capture the problems the person in this position fixes or the opportunities
they take advantage of. Look at things that would not happen right without
the right person in the job.

What. Align on what they should deliver – their
objectives/goals/outcomes. Objectives are general. Goals and outcomes
are specific. Together those comprise what they are accountable for.

How in general. Lay out organizational relationships, authority &
interdependencies. Capture superiors, peers, subordinates and others they
need to work with. Clarify what decisions they can make and how they
work interdependently with others and their impact on the rest of the
organization – how others' work/lives will be made better by them.

Specifically, how. Dig into the activities or things they need to do on the
way to delivering the objectives, goals, outcomes in a way that impacts the
rest of the organization – their specific responsibilities. Include areas in
which they consult with others and provide or receive input.

So, what. As a bonus, think through your picture of success for the role –
your vision for how things will look different when they have done what is
needed. It's sometimes helpful to imagine yourself taking this person out
for a celebratory dinner two years in and saying "You must be so proud of
the way you…."

Note these ideas are pulled from our Recruiting Brief tool and are
applicable to a whole range of positions beyond just VPs. Click here to
request a free copy.

Title

Now you know enough to figure out their title. Look for a title that helps
them do their job. Pick a title that communicates their remit – the problem
they should fix. Pick a title that helps others inside and outside the
organization figure out how to interact with them. This is where level
comes in. Worry less about communicating the specific responsibilities.
Those you can fill in later and they will evolve over time.

How Joe Biden (And You) Can Keep Those Not Selected as VP Engaged

Elizabeth Warren not chosen as VP AFP via Getty Images

The Democrats will nominate Kamala Harris as Vice President this week. At the same time, there are more people that wanted the job and thought they had at least an outside chance than any of us imagine. Biden needs to keep them engaged and needs to do that with emotional, rational and inspirational communication – as do you with people you do not select for plum assignments.

Who thought they had a chance?

The list of those thinking they had a chance is large. There are people that were on the final short list, on the long list, those directly considered, indirectly considered, thought they should be considered, contributed time, money or support to Biden in different ways. The point is that whether or not Biden actively considered them, there are a lot of people, female and male, who still thought they had an outside chance.

Emotional

While some may be relieved, most are disappointed. Biden and team need to acknowledge and deal with those emotions first– for more than just the finalists. Biden has to notice, acknowledge and empathize with them, know that their disappointment makes sense, and understand how their feelings. People need to feel seen and heard before they can connect. Affirming that their feelings makes sense tells them Biden is still on their side. Digging into understand their feelings even better tells them Biden cares.

Biden started doing this by reaching out to the finalists himself, one-on-one to do what Alexander Burns describes as "the hard business of letting down the runners-up that he had come to value as allies and friends." This was the right thing to do on all sorts of different levels. The general advice for an announcement cascade is to tell those emotionally impacted one-on-one first, then those directly impacted in a small group, then everyone else.

Rational

People want truth. They want truth from people that notice and acknowledge them, think they make sense and care about them. But they want truth. The truth will be different for different people not selected for VP now.

- Some were ready, but did not fit Biden's particular criteria. Biden can help them understand that in a way that makes them walk away with their head held high in line with this being "a career elevation for everybody."
- Some weren't ready yet. Biden can help them understand what must change either in the world or in themselves for them to be the right choice in the future.
- Some are never going to be the right choice. Biden can help them understand why that is the case and how their strengths are more applicable in other roles.

Inspirational

Having connected emotionally, and hit them with the brutal hard truth, Biden needs to inspire them to move forward. On the one hand Biden needs their support. On the other hand, the country and world need their support. On still another hand, they need a path for their own further contribution for their own self-esteem.

This is where the levels of engagement come in.

- If Biden tells them what to do (or you tell people what to do,) the best you can ever hope for is compliance – a limiting concept.
- If Biden sells them on a different path for them, tests it with them, or gives them an initial idea to build on, he increases the likelihood of their contributions.
- If Biden co-creates the future with them, they will commit to the cause.

Let's go a little deeper on committing to the cause. In this case, there's a problem and an opportunity. A lot of people are committed to doing anything that can to make sure Trump does not have a second terms. For them, Trump is the problem. Others care about the programs the democratic party is pushing. For them, moving those programs forward is the opportunity.

In either case, it's less about Biden than it is about Trump or the Democratic programs. The point is that Biden and you should focus less on getting people committed to him or you as the leader and more on getting them committed to the cause because the cause is more important than either themselves or the one wrong mistake Biden or you made in not picking them as VP.

August 25

The Mindset Change Required to Make Virtual Team Rooms Work

Team room Getty Images

A long time ago in a galaxy far, far away, people worked together in the same physical space. They could all look at the same things in the same dimension at the same time and use words, tone and body language to communicate. Now workers are scattered all over the universe and suffer from the associated barriers to communicating and working together. Many of the highest functioning teams have substituted virtual team rooms for physical team rooms. Making that work requires both a technical solution and a mindset of mutual support.

N.B. This applies only to teams - people with complementary strengths, committed to each other, working interdependently to realize a shared purpose. Work groups that do not have to work interdependently don't need this.

You will need a technical platform for your virtual team room. It could be as simple as Basecamp, which CTOs seem to rave about, Google docs, Office 365/Sharepoint, Trello, Mavenlink, or one of the various collaboration tools rated here. The best tools will facilitate accountability and cohesiveness.

You will also need a mindset change. For some of you, the most important attitude shift is from taking criticism as an attack to assuming positive intent from a teammate trying to contribute to your own personal growth and success.

Let's look at the four components of a high-performing team I just suggested:

Complementary strengths: Forget everything you've ever heard about a team being only a strong as its weakest link. That's only true if team members don't back each other up and fill each other's gaps with their complementary strengths. Complementary strengths are only complementary if they balance a complementary weakness. Otherwise they're redundant strengths.

Committed to each other: Katzenbach and Smith first made this point over 25 years ago in The Wisdom of Teams. They argued the fundamental difference between working groups and teams is interdependence. Then, the difference between a "Real Team" and a "High Performance Team" is that they are "deeply committed to each other's personal growth and success."

Working interdependently: Football's New England Patriots' quarterback Tom Brady makes just that point. His passes are useless until his teammates catch them. And they don't even get thrown without protection from the front line. Professional singles tennis players are independent on the court. Professional quarterbacks only succeed if their teams succeed.

Realize a shared purpose: This purpose should be meaningful and rewarding. It should be good for others, leverage the team's combined strengths so the team as a whole is good at it, and be good for the team.

That mindset allows the team to leverage the value of team room or virtual team room tools. Here is one approach. Whatever platform you choose will have its own tools and forms. Use those. Just make sure they accomplish the same things guided by a team leader and project manager.

Start with three boards: 1) a plan board, 2) an insights board, and 3) an action board.

PLAN Board
Mission
Vision
Objectives
Goals
Strategies
Guiding Principles

Plan Board Bradt

The Plan Board won't change. It's there to remind everyone about the shared purpose. It's there to remind everyone about the shared purpose.

INSIGHTS Board
Conditions
Capabilities
Customers
Collaborators
Competitors

Insights Board Bradt

The Insights Board captures ever-improving and evolving insights about the key players and the situation.

ACTION Board					
Milestones			**Status**		
Action	Due Date	Accountable	Do/Doing/Done (Color code green/yellow/red)	Hang-ups/Requests for help	Inputs/Ideas/Offers to Help
Communication					
Who (target)	What			When	Media
Parking Lot					
Parked ideas					
Future Milestones					

Action Board Bradt

The Action Board is the heart of the game and includes:

Milestones – Action, due date, accountable

Status – Do/doing/done (perhaps with green/yellow/red highlighting to make it easy to see where things are going well and less well; hang-ups/requests for help; inputs/ideas/offers to help

Communication – Who (target), what, when, media.

Parking Lot – Parked ideas, future milestones

This board is continually updated – at meetings and between meetings. It should always have the most current information. Important team meetings should be held around this board live or virtually so everyone is looking at the same things at the same time cohesively.

Net, the team room, virtual team room and its Plan, Insight and Action boards help teams communicate, collaborate and deliver together.

Why Managing Hand-offs Is the Most Essential Skill for A High Performing Team

chef-waiter hand-off AFP via Getty Images

When some teams of high performers don't quite gel, it's due to breakdowns in communication. Each member may have the strengths required. They may mean well. But they're not working well together. Look to the points of intersection, the hand-offs for the fix.

Recently, I was at a concert reading for a new musical. At one point, there was an awkward pause. It seemed like one of the actors had forgotten his lines. But it was a reading. He literally had the full script in front of him. Then it dawned on me. The director had had another actor modify one of her lines. The actor looking awkward hadn't forgotten his own lines. His cue had changed and he didn't know it.

You've seen the same thing with missed passes in sport matches and with missed cues, passes and hand-offs in organizations. A perfect pass is only perfect when paired with a perfect catch.

The old total quality SIPOC tool applies. It suggests that all work is a process with inputs from suppliers and outputs to customers.

Supplier => Input => Process => Output => Customer

Assuming you've got the right people in the right roles with the right direction and training, breakdowns happen at the hand-offs. Things go badly when the supplier is not clear on what inputs the process owner needs at what time in what way or when the process owner is not clear on what outputs the customer needs at what time in what way.

SIPOC works for those collaborating, but not necessarily as a team. One tool that can make the hand-offs work better is briefing documents. Briefing documents help clarify specific, one-off deliverables. Time invested in briefing documents and specifications reduces errors and re-work from missed hand-offs later.

General briefing document

- Lay out the context for the work, taking into consideration customers, collaborators, capabilities, competitors and conditions as appropriate.
- Clarify the objectives, fitting specific project objectives within the organization's overall purpose to make it clear how this work fits within the broader picture.
- Be definite on policies that must be followed and guidelines that may be followed in guiding how the work is completed.
- Specify mandatory executional elements and deliverables.
- Agree timeline for what gets delivered to whom, when, and how.

It's different for teams. The fundamental difference between a work group and a team is that members of a work group, like a law firm, may or may not collaborate on any specific work. Each member is fully capable of completing their own work. Members of an interdependent team cannot complete their work without help from other members on the team.

For example, the case team within a law firm may consist of a client relationship partner to work with the client, a researcher to investigate things, and a litigator to argue the case in court. These three have complementary strengths and must work together.

Teams with strong tactical capacity can work under difficult, changing conditions to translate strategies into tactical actions decisively, rapidly, and effectively. These teams empower each member and communicate effectively to come up with critical solutions to the inevitable problems that arise on an ongoing basis and to implement them quickly. Their hand-offs are flexible, clean and decisive.

Strong teams

Work together to build a common understanding of the context for the work, taking into consideration customers, collaborators, capabilities, competitors and conditions as appropriate.

Co-create shared objectives, fitting specific project objectives within the organization's overall so all know how any work fits within the broader picture.

Have a bias to flexible guidelines over hard and fast policies that must be followed so they can adjust to new learning on a continual basis.

Put themselves in each other's shoes as they think through executional elements and deliverables.

Generally operate well in advance of timelines for what gets delivered to whom, when, and how with clean, almost seamless hand-offs.

September 8

Taking A Page Out of Drew Bees' Playbook to Lead Through COVID-19

Drew Brees leading Getty Images

It's one thing to break the single season passing NFL passing record after it stood for 27 years. It's a whole other thing to lead through a pandemic. Or is it? Walk-On's Sports Bistreaux's leaders Brandon Landry and Scott Taylor have reapplied Drew Brees' leadership philosophy to their business – as they should. Brees was the guy who broke that record and is a co-owner and partner in their business.

Brees' locker room speech after breaking Dan Marino's record on December 27, 2011 is a masterclass in respectful leadership, hitting on empathy, authenticity, innovation, values and inspiration. There's no false modesty here. He's just clear that <u>we</u> had this opportunity "because of the guys in this room" – all of them: players, coaches, equipment managers, trainers. He goes on to talk about all the people that caught passes in all sorts of innovative ways. He talks about teamwork and pride. He points the way to their journey filled with an even brighter future.

https://www.youtube.com/watch?v=AuaaXRAY2Ls

Hopefully Brees has been applying that same attitude and approach to today's controversies.

In any case, Walk-On's Scott Taylor took me through how they apply these ideas at Walk-On's. While the full-service restaurant industry was flipped on its head amid the pandemic, Taylor credits their leadership culture for successfully adapting business operations, retaining staff, continuing to open new restaurants, and sign multi-unit agreements as COVID-19 rages on. As Taylor explained,

Strengthened Empathy: While always central to exceptional leadership, the pandemic created a crash course on how empathy should be the primary, guiding principle to anyone's leadership style. The emotion brought forth by the pandemic is felt by all – leaders are faced to understand and navigate how that impacted their teams, motivation and productivity.

Walk-On's has used more 1:1 meetings/access to leadership, all-new work from home policies, and even started diversity task forces as the nation has faced social unrest. By prioritizing empathy and gaining perspective, Walk-On's leaders are making better decisions more quickly than ever before.

Straightforward Authenticity: The pandemic is forcing leaders to embrace vulnerability and showcase a new level of authenticity. Walk-On's leaders are sharing issues, discussing what they're struggling with, asking for help, being transparent.

When you do this, your team will too, and together you can work toward creative solutions more effectively and efficiently (i.e. how to shift business model in COVID world, how to keep all staff employed with no furloughs, how to repair relationships after taking controversial stands on issues, etc.).

Refined Focus on Innovation: The pandemic is forcing leaders to be aggressive vs. conservative when it comes to innovation. Whether it is the use of new technology, AI, social distance-friendly models, new products/services, or an all new arm of the business, the pandemic has brought forth a new wave of innovation.

Walk-On's leaders had to accelerate their long-term goals, adjust, and push forward – realizing the value in not only preparing for the future, but acting on it sooner.

Core Values Take Precedence: Amid the chaos, Walk-On's leaders relied heavily on brand core values that unified employees and kept fear in check. Shared values inspired accountability and served as a reality check for coming together and trucking the through mud to prevail and overcome the pandemic.

With strengthened core values, Walk-On's leaders have been able to build teams with the right people in the right seats to actualize the company purpose – just like Brees did with the Saints.

Being Inspirational is a Requirement: Walk-On's strong leaders quickly understood that while the pandemic controlled many aspects of their business, one thing it could not rob them of was their mindset. Walk-On's team members needed their leaders to have a fierce, positive, resilient mindset. People were scared to death, but whether it was daily emails, 1:1 zoom meetings, mental health checks, etc., employees needed the reminder and the encouragement that "this is a moment in time, not the end of time" to give them inspiration to carry on and contribute in their role.

As Brees put it, "That's the journey we're on. And it's going to be about us as we continue on, as we win next week, and we continue to win and we continue this journey."

There are so many unknowns. As you help people accept the darkest parts of the current reality, deal with controversies, and move forward where they can and how they can step-by-step, and yard-by-yard, do lead with empathy, authenticity, innovation, values and inspiration.

September 10

How Naming Jane Fraser CEO Advances Citibank's Client Focus

Newly named CEO of Citibank - Jane Fraser © 2019 Bloomberg Finance LP

Ultimately, all banks are in the client service business. Their product, money, is the ultimate commodity in that its value is literally written on its face. While that can design new services, and enroll interesting partners, they ultimately win or lose based on the quality of their clients' experiences. Citibank recruited, developed and has now named Jane Fraser as its next CEO to give them an advantage in that area.

Citi's Michael Klein spent "several years" trying to get Fraser to join Citibank, finally succeeding in 2004. He did this not because of her experience at Goldman Sachs, Asesores Bursátiles, or McKinsey, not because of her Harvard MBA, but because of what she had learned researching and writing her book, "Race for the World: Strategies to Build a Great Global Firm."

What she had learned was empathy.

She researched this book by traveling around the world and interviewing McKinsey clients about their challenges. At the same time, she was working part time to spend time with her young children. The combination gave her a rare perspective range from global to as personal as it gets.

Then Citi moved her through a series of positions that allowed her to build knowledge and skills, heading up client strategy, mergers and acquisitions, the Private Bank, CitiMortgage, US Consumer and Commercial Banking, Citigroup Latin America, Global Consumer Banking.

She'll take over as CEO with the talent, knowledge and skills required to steer the bank out of the pandemic and through the uncertain future we all have to deal with.

Different CEOs for different needs.

There are all sorts of good lessons here. You have to be impressed with the way Jane Fraser has managed her career. You have to be impressed with the way she balanced her family and work. You have to be impressed with Michael Klein spotting her talent and sticking with it to convince her to join Citi. You have to be impressed with the way Citi nurtured her.

And you have to be impressed with Citi's matching the person and the task. Fraser is a great choice for CEO of a service company. She would be less valuable in a design, production or distribution-focused company.

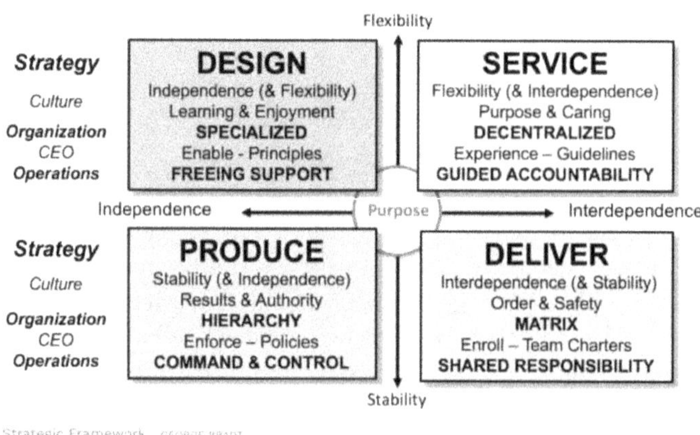

The "E" in CEO is different for different companies.

Design

If your organization is design-focused, like Apple, you win by out-innovating your competition. The CEO has to be the Chief Enabler. They have to give the most important people in the company – the designers – freeing support.

The CEO's job is to protect those designers from all the corporate weenies trying to restrict their freedom. The CEO will do battle on behalf of the designers with a never-ending parade of lawyers, accountants and engineers constantly trying to limit the damage those designers do. Because, of course, innovation requires damaging the status quo.

Produce

If your organization is production-focused, like coal mining companies, you win by being more efficient than your competition. The CEO has to be the Chief Enforcer. They have to make sure everyone follows the policies.

In some ways, this is the most straightforward of all CEO roles as these organizations operate best with command and control hierarchies. The CEO sits at the top, dictates policies, pushes stability and makes sure things happen the same way every time.

Deliver

If your organization is delivery-focused, like Amazon, you win by building a better network. The CEO has to be the Chief Enroller, bringing people into the network.

The challenge here is that the matrix, by definition, includes people outside the company. The CEO has no control. They have to push interdependence. They have to drive shared responsibility.

Service

If your organization is service-focused, like Citibank, you win on the dimension of customer experience. The CEO has to be the Chief Experience Officer, guiding decentralized service providers.

The key words here are guided accountability. Each customer and client is different. Each has a different experience. They judge organizations by the person providing them their service. So, the service providers need flexibility. But it needs to be guided to align with the organization's mission, vision and points of differentiation.

Different groups within any organization will have different remits. Citibank's compliance group is a production sub-group. Their job is to enforce policies. In some ways, all CEOs must be part enabler, part enforcer, part enroller, and part chief experience officer. Different CEOs just need to do those with different priorities.

September 15

How to Decide Which Role to Fill Next to Increase Your Organization's Effectiveness

Coordinating resources Toronto Star via Getty Images

If you want to get more done in the same amount of time you have to add resources. Every leader there ever was has faced the immutable law that scope is a function of resources and time. To get more done, you must add tools to make yourself and others more productive and add appropriate people in different roles to increase capacity. The role to fill next is the one that provides the most important and most urgent leverage – likely contributors, managers, coordinators, deputies, and then chiefs of staff in that order.

At a high level,

Leaders inspire and enable others to do their absolute best, together to realize a meaningful and rewarding shared purpose.

Deputies are second in command, empowered to act in their leader's absence.

Chiefs of Staff give leaders leverage by managing them, priorities, programs and projects, and communication.

Managers of units, functions, programs and projects directly manage pieces of the overall puzzle and are accountable for delivery of their unit, function, program or project's results.

Contributors work for unit, function, program or project managers and are responsible for delivering their own work.

Coordinators administratively coordinate others' efforts, but are neither accountable nor responsible – unless they are acting as program or project managers or contributors.

Regardless of title, people often wear different hats at different times.

One key is to understand each position's accountabilities. In general,

Accountable: Overall ownership of results. Drives decisions. Ensures implementation.

Responsible: Does defined work.

Consulted: Provides input.

Informed: Kept up-to-date. (One-way communication.)

Deputies are accountable for the decisions they make in their leader's absence.

Chiefs of Staff spend a lot of their time consulting and providing input, making others more efficient and effective across the enterprise.

Unit, function, program and project managers are accountable for delivering results in their areas and, in the spirit of bounded authority, make tactical decisions along the way.

Contributors are responsible for, wait for it, their contributions.

Coordinators spend their time communicating across the people within a project if they are the project coordinator or across projects if they are the program coordinator.

Now that you understand the difference between these various positions, how do you as a leader determine which you need next?

Contributors are your organization's muscle, actually doing the work. Build your muscle before you do anything else.

Managers of units, functions, programs and projects are the heart of your organization, translating overall direction into unit, functional, program and project priorities and managing delivery. These are generally the highest leverage additions once you have enough contributors.

Coordinators add leverage by working behind the scenes to arrange and coordinate resources.

Chiefs of Staff are all about leverage. Their primary function is managing your priorities and communication. In these they are consulting (two-way communication) and informing (one-way communication.) Additionally, they may pick up direct management for priorities, programs or projects. When they do that they look like a manager.

Deputies are all about succession planning, capacity and development.

Your deputy is generally your designated successor. This is particularly true if your deputy has "deputy" in their title. If you move out for any reason, they should be ready, willing and able to step into your position instantly.

Deputies give you, yourself increased leverage. Deputies often have the title of Chief Operating Officer. Those deputies give leader's increased leverage by managing operations. Alternately, your deputy could manage the organizational process (often with the title of Chief Human Resource Officer) or the strategic process (with titles like Chief Strategy Officer, CFO, CMO, General Counsel or others.)

You may choose to move someone into a deputy role to further their development. In this case, the deputy will not be your designated successor. Instead they could be being groomed for a different role. You might for example, transition a CFO from heading the finance function to serving as your overall deputy for a period of time to broaden their horizons before moving them into a business unit general management role.

Implications

Make sure everyone understands what their job is and is not, and how they should interact with others. In general, add contributors first to give you muscle and then unit, function, program and project managers to direct your contributors. Add coordinators to support them next. Then fill chief of staff and deputy roles to direct the managers.

September 22

What CEOs Must Do to Avoid The 83% Of Mergers and Acquisitions That Fail

Oracle -TikTok? Getty Images

The #1 job of a CEO is vision, values and culture. That true for mergers & acquisitions (M&A) as well. Owning the vision means making sure the tactical merger & acquisition choice matches the overarching company strategy. Owning the values and culture means making sure the merger or acquisition is culturally accretive.

Since 83% of mergers & acquisitions fail, we know most CEOs don't get this right. Coupling that with knowing that 70%+ of value creation for growth-oriented private equity firms comes from inorganic growth leads to the conclusion that those that do get this right reap oversized rewards.

Own the vision

If you as the CEO have M&A as a strategy you don't have a strategy. Mergers & acquisitions are not strategies. They are tactics. To be fair, they are very powerful tactics to accelerate through a strategic point of inflection. But if they aren't tactics in service to an overarching strategy, they are doomed to fail – as is the case 83% of the time.

As described in What it Takes to Accelerate Through a Strategic Inflection Point, there are only four over-arching strategies: design, produce, deliver and service.

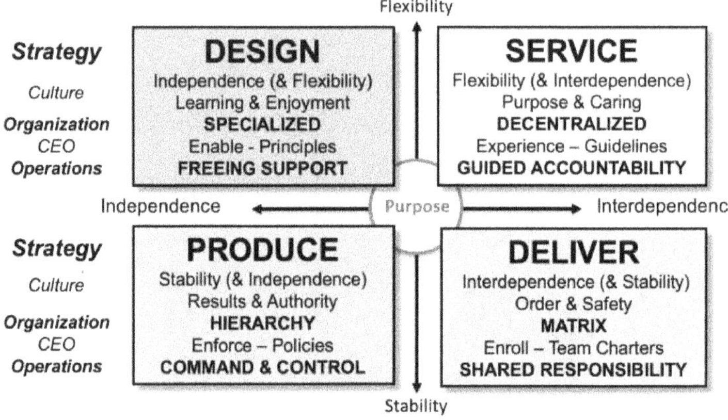

The only viable path to a successful merger & acquisition runs through one of those strategies.

- If your strategy is design, target mergers & acquisitions that enable design.
- If produce, target mergers & acquisitions that enforce production.
- If deliver, target mergers & acquisitions to enroll others in delivery – knowing that strategic alliances often work better here and always have less risk.
- If service, target mergers & acquisitions to enhance your customers' experience.

You're all nodding your heads thinking, "of course." Virtually all of the 17% of successful mergers & acquisitions start here. At the same time, one of the leading causes of failure for the 83% that fail is strategic mis-fit. So at least some of you are going to forget this lesson when offered an exciting merger or acquisition opportunity.

CEOs that forget this lesson get suckered in by pitches like:

"Complementary strengths" - which, almost by definition means they have a different strategy.

"Gives us scale" – valuable only if the scale fits your strategy or improves your structural economics to fuel your strategy.

"Access to new markets" – valuable only if the markets fit your strategy.

"New products" – valuable only if they fit your strategy.

Get the point? As CEO, own the vision. Own the mission. Own the strategy. Merge or buy only if it fits your strategy.

Own the culture

As I've written before, when you merge cultures well, value is created. When you don't, value is destroyed. Arguably, the root cause of every merger's success or failure is culture. The good news is that the path to merging cultures well is rooted in the strategic choice. So, if part I is targeting mergers & acquisitions that enhance your strategic choice, part II is targeting organizations that enhance both your strategy and culture.

At their essence,

- The most effective design-focused organizations have cultures of independence, learning and enjoyment. Lead them with principles as the chief enabler.
- Production-focused organizations have cultures of stability, results and authority. Lead them with policies as the chief enforcer.
- Delivery or distribution-focused organizations have cultures of interdependence, order and safety. Lead them with team charters as the chief enroller.
- Service-focused organizations have cultures of flexibility, purpose and caring. Lead them with guidelines as the chief experience officer.

Merge the cultures as soon as practical. If you don't think you need to integrate them, you shouldn't be merging them in or acquiring them in the first place.

Decide for each element of behaviors, relationships, attitude, values and environment which culture is going to survive, at least for the time being – yours, theirs, both, or a combination. Enroll leaders and team members from both sides of the acquisition in the process, so they know what the changes mean to them and they can be on their front foot, bringing their best to the integration.

Of course, this merger or acquisition will help you evolve your overall culture. You need to do that to lead through a strategic point of inflection. But do it deliberately, owning the new vision, values and culture yourself. That's how you avoid the 83% of mergers & acquisitions that fail.

September 23

How to Avoid the Self-Inflicted COVID Communication Disaster at JP Morgan Chase and Goldman Sachs

JP Morgan Chase, Goldman Sachs and Coronavirus SOPA Images/LightRocket via Getty Images

It's surprising and stunning that JP Morgan Chase and Goldman Sachs have got this so wrong. As CNBC reported, both banks' employees are learning about coronavirus cases in their buildings from press reports and not from their leaders. Their policies are "to inform only those who have been on the floor or who may have had contact with a sick person." The right approach to crisis management and crisis communication is to think in terms of physical safety, reputation and finances – in that order. These banks skipped step one, thereby hurting their reputations as well.

Here's why it's even more important to follow the right approach now:

Physical Safety First

COVID is still here. People are still scared. Everyone's first question about any change you're proposing (including re-opening your offices) is "What does this mean for me and my family?" If they don't believe you have their physical safety as your first priority, they're not going to hear anything else you have to say.

Putting people's safety first is not a choice. Do what you have to do to protect your team, customers and community. This is a classic "Be. Do. Say." leadership moment. No one is going to believe what you say about safety first unless your actions match your words. And if your words and actions don't match your fundamental, underlying beliefs, you will slip and you will get caught. No one is going to trust you as a leader unless you are trustworthy.

Not keeping people informed about COVID cases in their buildings was a violation of trust by JP Morgan Chase and Goldman Sachs. The ramifications are far greater and will be far more long-lasting than they realize. It will take a long time for the banks' leaders to re-earn the trust of their employees and their families.

What you should takeaway to avoid the self-inflicted COVID communication disaster at JP Morgan Chase and Goldman Sachs: Put physical safety first. Believe it matters. Act like it matters. Talk about it like it matters. In that order.

Reputation

There is no daylight between corporate or organizational reputation and leadership reputation. The leaders of poorly regarded organizations suffer reputational hits, and organizations with poorly regarded leaders suffer similar reputational hits.

There is also no daylight between internal and external communication anymore. As this example highlights, internal people read and share external news stories. And internal communication finds its way into external platforms instantly.

This is why these banks' policies of trying to compartmentalize information is so ludicrously out of date. There are no compartments. Information flows from one compartment inside the organization to people outside the organization and then back in.

What you should takeaway to avoid the self-inflicted COVID communication disaster at JP Morgan Chase and Goldman Sachs: Know that everything communicates. If there was ever a time to be consistent and transparent, it's now. Everything you say and do and don't say and don't do and everything anyone in your organization says and does and doesn't say and doesn't do will impact your organization's reputation and yours.

Crisis Management Framework

The essence of our proposed crisis management approach, per my earlier article on Learnings from Boeing's 737 Max, Coca-Cola and Procter & Gamble on Crisis Management, is all about inspiring and enabling others to get things vaguely right quickly, and then adapt along the way - with clarity around direction, leadership and roles.

1. PREPARE IN ADVANCE: The better you have anticipated possible scenarios, the more prepared you are, the more confidence you will have when crises strike.
2. REACT TO EVENTS: The reason you prepare is so that all can react quickly and flexibility to the situation they face. Don't over-think this. Let people do what they prepared to do.
3. BRIDGE THE GAPS. In a crisis, there is inevitably a gap between the desired and current state of affairs. Rectify that by bridging those gaps in the current situation, your response and ability to prevent future crises.

This is recapped in our Crisis Management tool. Click here to get a free copy or download it from www.onboardingtools.com.

Ultimately, what you're going to be left with after the crisis is your personal and brand reputation. Re-look at your brand values. Make sure you are protecting your core strategic planks. Treat all in a way that enhances your reputation with them. Over time, they'll remember how you treated them and how you made them feel at the worst moments.

October 1

Why Every Team Needs A Periodic Scrum – The Irreplaceable Value of Live Meetings

Opening Scrum Sygma via Getty Images

Not every working group needs to meet live. That's because not every working group needs to function as a team. Many working groups can do fine working mostly <u>independently</u>, coordinating communication and learning as appropriate. By definition, teams are made up of individuals who must work <u>interdependently</u> to achieve a mutual objective. For them, consensus rules. And the best tool for building consensus is live, real time meetings.

The New Yorker's Cal Newport asked <u>Was e-mail a Mistake</u>? He suggests it was not, given its value in asynchronous communication allowing receivers to read the senders' messages whenever convenient for the receivers. At the same time, it is less effective for "The consensus problem" and other things requiring synchronized, real time communication. One of the examples he cites is tech companies' "Scrums" – 15 minute daily stand-up meetings to collaboratively set up each day's work.

As the world continues to flatten with people working whenever they want, wherever they want, it gets harder and harder to collaborate and coordinate work. There will, of course, be an ever-increasing flow of collaborative tools. And you should use the ones that work best for you. The warning is to be clear on when you need a team and how you're going to enable those team members' essential interdependence.

The importance of <u>non-verbal communication</u> comes into play here as well. At least in some specific instances, about 7% of communication is the words. About 38% comes through tone. And 55% comes through body language. One of the problems with email is that it's tone-deaf. All you get is the words. No tone. No body language. Phone calls pick up tone. And video-conferencing picks up body language. You're still missing the ability to be in the same room, breathing the same air as people with whom you're trying to collaborate.

Coordinating communication across independent members of working groups can happen virtually. While they should likely meet from time to time to build relationships and connections, those meetings are not essential for working groups. On the other hand, interdependent teams need periodic meetings in line with the nature of the problems they deal with.

Team Remit	Meeting Frequency
Strategic	Annual
Core Process	Quarterly
Program-level	Monthly
Project-level	Weekly
Task-level	Daily
Crisis-management	Each shift

Strategic Remit

Teams with strategic remits are charged with looking at the long-term. They could be advisory councils and the like. Because they are thinking in terms of years or decades, they need to meet only annually or even less frequently.

Core Process Remit

Core process teams manage or guide an organization's core strategic, organizational and operating processes. They could be boards of directors or an expanded management team. It's helpful for them to meet live on a regular quarterly basis, perhaps dealing with their remits on schedules that like this:

- Q1 – Talent Reviews
- Q2 – Strategic Planning (with the strategic advisory council)
- Q3 – Future Capability Planning
- Q4 – Operating Plans

Program Remit

Programs are the bridge between strategies and projects. As such, it's helpful for programs to be managed more frequently than quarterly, but less frequently than weekly – say monthly.

Project Remit

Project teams need to get together live at least once a week for joint-problem solving and direction setting.

Task Remit

Tasks are the day-to-day, front-line work. If all you need from the workers is compliance, you don't really need to meet with them on a regular basis as each person can focus on their own task. But, if you want those workers to contribute as a team, they need to meet as a team at least daily like they do in tech companies' scrums.

Crisis Management

The core of good crisis management is the prepare – react – bridge cycle. Ideally, you prepare in advance of a crisis. Then you are reacting to unfolding events and constantly bridging the gaps between the current reality and desired state. This rapid-cycling requires core crisis management teams to meet live at least at the beginning of each shift.

Implications for you

Make each team's remit clear. Guide them into the right cadence of meetings – in line with their remits. Ensure the meet live as appropriate to spend time together to strengthen their ability to work interdependently.

Helping Employees Manage Through COVID Wave II

Inmates recaptured AFP via Getty Images

COVID-19 reset everyone's progress up Maslow's hierarchy of physiological, safety, belonging, self-esteem, and self-actualization needs. As you helped your employees re-boot through the first wave of the pandemic, you needed to meet them where they were and move back up the hierarchy together. It's even harder as people go through wave II and go through the same steps again.

Maslow Hygiene Factors

In general, the first two levels of Maslow's hierarchy are what Frederick Herzberg described as hygiene factors. People's physiological and safety needs need to be met well enough for them not to be problems. If they're not met well enough, the higher-level needs are irrelevant. But they are pass-fail gates. There's no advantage to meeting them better than well enough.

The top levels are satisfiers. The more self-esteem and self-actualization, the better.

Belonging benefits are caught in the middle. They are higher-level than hygiene factors, but often not satisfiers on their own. People want to belong to a club, tribe, or fan base. But it's only a differentiating benefit if that membership builds their self-esteem or self-actualization.

The First Re-boot

One of the tricky things for organizations in the early days of the pandemic was the shift from focusing on Maslowian satisfiers to hygiene. The issue is that people generally move through Maslow's hierarchy sequentially. They can't even think about the next level up until they've satisfied the level below. And the pandemic sent everyone back to thinking about physiological or safety needs. This creates two traps for organizations:

Trap #1 is not meeting people where they are. You can't get people to focus on the company's purpose when they are trying to figure out how to pay for their next meal.

Trap #2 is applying higher order satisfier thinking to hygiene factors. The return on investment to be the safest place to work isn't there. Employers should invest what it takes to be safe enough. Then, invest in differentiating employee benefits like experience.

The Second Re-boot

It's even harder the second time around for a couple of reasons. 1) Stress is cumulative. The longer this goes on, the more stressful it is for all. 2) People are dealing with the effects of psychological torture in prison.

Don't kid yourself. For some, the pandemic has shifted their work-life balance. They don't have to commute or travel, and can spend more time with their families, friends, pets and house plants. For others, the pandemic has been a prison sentence, cutting them off from social interactions and trapping them in confined spaces – sometimes with people with whom they would rather not share a cell.

Unfortunately, now it's even worse than that. One way to torture prisoners is to let them think they've escaped all the while setting a trap to recapture them. It's a way to get them to give up hope and accept the futility of resistance. Some who saw the pandemic as a prison sentence have seen the relaxation of restrictions as an escape. They are not going to take the reinstatement of restrictions and their recapture well.

Implications for you

Take a hard re-look at your employees and where they are playing on Maslow's hierarchy now. Be on the lookout for their having dropped back to concerns about safety or physiological needs – especially if they had experienced a relaxation of restrictions.

Meet your target where they are now. In most cases, this will mean focusing on and communicating your physiological and safety standards first. Don't over-promise. No one knows how the pandemic is going to play out and when there will be safe and effective vaccines. Overpromising is like giving prisoners false hope. It will hurt them and your relationship with them over time.

One key here is going to distributed story crafting and storytelling. Physiological and safety needs are highly emotional. The most emotionally resonant communication is one-on-one. If you're leading a large organization, find ways to help others throughout the organization get physiological and safety wins and tell others about them one-on-one. You can't be everywhere. But you can help others amplify your influence.

Then play to win, investing in and communicating belonging, self-esteem or self-actualization benefits as we finally do get through the pandemic.

October 13

Executive Onboarding with A Boss Who Didn't Want You

Frustrated boss Getty Images

It happens all the time. Headquarters or owners drops someone in to help a division or portfolio company accelerate through a point of inflection, working for a boss who doesn't want them. If you're the one getting dropped in, emphasize building trust in the face of possible distrust or resentment. Jump-shift your loyalties immediately. 1) Disengage from your previous situation; 2) Engage with your new boss; and 3) Do what is required to accelerate progress – in that order.

Disengage

Be prepared for your new boss to fear the worst. They may think you're there to spy on them, to shore up one of their personal weaknesses, or to replace them. As much as they try to bury those concerns, and whether they voice them or not, they are real and must be addressed before they can trust you.

Your long-term loyalty to the people that put you in to work for your new boss is best served by transferring your immediate loyalty from them to your new boss. Help them by helping your new boss. Make this is a hard shift. You no longer work for the people you used to work for. You work for your new boss and have to earn their trust. The best way to earn trust is to be trustworthy.

Be explicit with the people that put you into the job. Be clear that you're going to route communication to them through your new boss. Neither they nor you should go around your new boss in any way. You may not be able to and may not want to sever all communication links, but you can make sure your new boss knows everything you're telling their bosses – ideally before you tell them. And in all cases make sure your new boss hears about communication with their bosses from you and not from them.

Engage

Choose to be optimistic. Believe the best about your new boss and how you can help them get done what they need to get done. Even if they didn't choose to have you work for them, you can choose to make this the best possible experience with the best possible results for all involved. Focus on these positives at all times with all people in all your thoughts, words and actions.

Leave your ego at the door. Proactively tell your new boss that you want to be part of their team. Commit to your new team's purpose - its cause. Do this explicitly with your words. Then follow up with actions to reinforce this.

Adjust to your new boss' working style immediately. This is a hard shift, not an evolution around control points, decision-making and communication.

Engage with your boss personally. Make them feel appreciated, valued and valuable. Invest to learn what matters to them and why. Learn their stories. Learn about them and from them.

Create and present your new boss with a realistic and honest game plan to get up to speed on your new organization. Don't assume that what the people that dropped you in told you or what you observed from your previous vantage point was right. Look at things with a fresh pair of eyes as though you were joining the organization for the first time. Seek out your new boss's perspective early and often, and be open to new directions.

One key to engaging is to put the relationship with your new boss first – as much as you can without becoming a victim of their battles with others.

Accelerate

Understand and move on your new boss' agenda immediately. Know your boss' priorities. Know what your new boss thinks your priorities should be. Be open and willing to do whatever it takes to move the organization forward, putting aside your own interests as appropriate.

Be on your "A" game. Be present and "on" – everything done by you and your team will be part of your new boss' evaluation of you. Deliver early wins that are important to your new boss and to the people they listen to, showing that you are 100% behind your boss. In a restart, the score is reset. Your old wins and your team's old wins are history. This is a reset and a whole new opportunity to accelerate.

Know there are going to be bumps in the road. Adjust as required to minor or major surprises with temporary or enduring impact.

Be. Do. Say. The Foundation of Authentic, Trusted Leadership

Responding to an accident Los Angeles Times via Getty Images

In their town, deep in the last century, the paramedics and emergency medical technicians that staffed the life squad's ambulance were volunteers. They were on call for twelve-hour shifts and carried beepers so they could be summoned whatever they were doing.

He was on call and at home when he heard an accident on the corner.

He ran down to see if people needed help and he found a two-car accident. So, he secured the victims as best he could, got some bystanders to put one of the victims in traction, and got others to call the police and life squad and tell them he was on site and needed help.

When the rest of the life squad showed up, they packaged up the victims, safely transported them to the hospital and returned to the life squad building to clean the ambulance and restock it for its next call.

The life squad captain walked in and addressed him.

"I noticed you were on the scene of that accident without your red jacket on."

Life squad jackets ullstein bild via Getty Images

"Yes. I was. I had been at home, working in my front yard. I heard the accident and ran straight there to help as quickly as I could. I leave my jacket in my car when I'm on duty."

"I understand. But you should take the extra time and get your jacket. Its visibility helps keep you safe on site and helps you control the scene."

"You're absolutely right. My mistake. Won't do it again."

He turned to go back to his work.

Then he stopped.

"How did you notice I was on the scene without my jacket?"

"I drove by."

"I'm sorry. You drove by the scene of a two-car accident close enough and slowly enough to notice that I wasn't wearing my jacket? You must have noticed that I was the only one on the scene. I could have used some help."

Let's be clear on this, the captain was right to enforce the jacket policy. Her logic made total sense. The issue was that her actions were not in line with the squad's mission. Every life squad there ever was and ever will be has had and will have a mission of providing emergency medical care.

In an earlier article on the Red Cross's Charley Shimanski, we looked at his story of people in a restaurant who hear the sound of a significant car accident. As he describes it,

- Many will go to the window to see what happened.
- Some will go to the curb to see what happens next.
- But a small number of those patrons will rush to the accident scene to BE what happens next - helping out however they can to the best of their abilities.

The Red Cross are second responders. They support first responders and victims. Life Squads are first responders. Their mission is to "rush to the accident scene to BE what happens next – helping out however they can to the best of their abilities."

Implications for you

Not suggesting you have to rush to accident scenes – unless you're the captain of a life squad. But your actions must match your words and your underlying beliefs if you're going to have any credibility as a leader.

No one's going to believe your words, what you say. Talk is cheap.

People will believe what you do.

Pick your cliché. Walk the talk. Practice what you preach. That's table stakes.

But if your actions match your words without matching your fundamental underlying beliefs, you will slip up and you will get caught.

Be. Do. Say. Starts with "Be." Make sure you truly believe in your organization's mission and values. If you do, it's easy to talk about it. Just say what comes naturally. If you do, let your actions flow from those underlying beliefs.

If you don't fundamentally believe in your organization's mission, get out. There may be some short-term benefits to staying for a while. You may be able to learn new things. You may be able to practice new skills. You may get valuable recognition and rewards.

But you can't be the best leader you can be unless everything about you inspires and enables others to do their absolute best together to realize a meaningful and rewarding shared purpose. You'll drive by accidents until you're the accident yourself.

October 22

Three Pieces of Advice from Moody's Outgoing CEO, Ray McDaniel

Raymond McDaniel - BLOOMBERG NEWS

Ray McDaniel came to a CEO Boot Camp on his fifth day as CEO in 2005. He came back to a dinner before another Boot Camp six years later to answer the question "What do you wish you'd known then that you know now?" He said three things:

1. "I wish I had known the world was about to blow up." Moody's had systemically rated companies credit way too high going into the 2008-2009 downturn.
2. "I wish I'd known that companies get mad when you downgrade their credit ratings, but when you downgrade countries' credit ratings, they raid your offices and put your people in jail."
3. "I wish I'd known how much fun it was to testify in front of Congress. I would have called in sick." Congress people don't so much ask you questions as use you as an excuse to make whatever points they need to make to their constituents.

Moody's just announced that Robert Fauber will take over as CEO from McDaniel effective January 1, 2021. Now McDaniel can tell Fauber what he wished someone had told him in 2005. He could give Fauber three envelopes or he could take the same general advice that he wish he had given to himself and apply it to today's circumstances. Those morph into:

1. The world has blown up and will never be the same.
2. Think beyond companies and beyond countries to cross-border players.
3. Testifying in front of congress is fun. (Not.)

The world has blown up and will never be the same

Anyone that tells you they know how Covid-19 is going to play out is either lying, delusional, running for President, or all three. But here's what we do know:

Covid-19 is one of the seminal events of all our lives.

Almost everything is disrupted.

All the king's horses and all the king's men won't be able to put the world back together again resembling what it was in any shape or form.

Covid-19 is arguable the mother of all Black Swan events, not so much in that it's a massive Black Swan event itself (which it is,) but in that it is going to give birth to a whole generation of Black Swan events.

We're living in a word in which one of the most successful CEO's of our time, Meg Whitman, can go through almost $2B and effectively bankrupt streaming platform Quibi in six months.

We're living in a world experiencing one of the biggest transfers of wealth between the winners and the losers since Rome conquered the known world.

Fauber needs take all this into account as he and his team try to help others navigate financial markets.

Think beyond companies and beyond countries to cross-border players.

In some ways, McDaniel had it easy. While he couldn't predict how different countries were going to react to what Moody's did, at least he knew where the countries were. Fauber's going to have to deal with cross-border players like Google and Facebook and Alibaba and Tencent that have shown a complete disregard for individual countries' rules, locating their operations wherever best suits them and moving them at the drop of a Bitcoin.

It's hard to rate companies' credit when you can't pin down their locations.

Fauber and his team need to figure out news ways of evaluating companies as the rules constantly evolve.

Testifying in front of congress is fun

Well, that advice from 2011 still holds. The divide in congress is deeper and more challenging than it ever was. Look at Amy Coney Barrett's hearings in front of the Judicial Committee. Steven Covey must be turning in his grave. He suggested we should "Seek First to Understand, Then to

Be Understood." None of the questions were designed to help people understand Judge Barrett. They were all designed to make points to future voters.

Fauber's not going to change the political realities Moody has to deal with. But he does need to understand them and take them into account.

McDaniel was right then; and he's still right. Fauber, and each of us, should be aware of the ever-changing nature of our world, look beyond our own narrow horizons, and learn to accept what we cannot change.

October 27

More on Mitigating the Risks of Onboarding into A Smaller Organization

Canoe Captain Portland Press Herald via Getty Images

If changing organizations for most people is like driving from Ethiopia to Kenya, for an executive onboarding from a large corporate to a smaller organization it's like the difference between driving a cruise ship and a row boat. In both cases, their instincts are wrong. In the first case they need to switch sides of the road to avoid head-on collisions. In the second case they need to pick up an oar if they want to move at all.

40% of new leaders fail in their first 18 months. They fail because of poor fit, poor delivery, or poor ability to adjust to changes down the road. As described in an earlier article, if you're an executive onboarding into smaller organizations you must:

- Fit within the organization's broader ecosystem as well as your workgroup
- Deliver with fewer resources and less structure
- Create change instead of waiting for it to happen

Make a hard shift to fit in

Fitting in is a non-trivial event. You have to be accepted by the team and become part of the team before you can ever hope to evolve it. Remember that most change agents don't survive their own changes. Understand the new culture and change your approach to fit in. In particular, be ready for these differences:

Expect a different environment

Corporate offices tend to signal power and status. Big, important corporations have big, important headquarters. Important and powerful corporate executives have big, impressive offices – the closer to the center of power the better.

Smaller organizations tend to be closer to the founder's garage. They care more about customers and colleagues than they do about physical space.

Net, any moment you spend worrying about your office - its size, shape, location, or décor – before or after you start is not just a moment wasted. It's a moment driving a wedge between you and them.

Expect a much more intimate relationship with values

Recently, many corporations have spent time reconnecting with their values. Some like Volkswagen, had gotten way off track. Some like HP forgot their founders' way. Not only are smaller entrepreneurial and family ventures closer to their founder's garage, they're made up of people who know or knew the founder and helped the founder develop their collective founding values. They don't need plaques on the wall engraved with values. They are the values. Learn the values by getting to know the people.

Expect a more cohesive attitude

Big corporations sprawl. They push the edges and either become or start to look like conglomerates. They have groups, division, units and sub-units, strategies and sub-strategies. Smaller, more entrepreneurial and family companies tend to be more focused. They still know what they have to do to survive. Figure out the core focus and focus your efforts there.

Expect more personal relationships

As corporations get larger, they get more distant and formal. They communicate more and more with memoranda, big documents and formal presentations. People in smaller organizations still talk to each other. Relationships matter equally in all organizations. They're just more equal in smaller entrepreneurial and family organizations – especially with family members or "friends" of the founder or family.

Expect less talk and more action

Big corporations get to protect all the good things they've built. Many times, the cost of a mistake is far greater than the potential gain from an action. They think things through to anticipate and mitigate all the risks. Smaller organizations are much more focused on potential with less to lose. Expect a bias to action. Have a bias to pick up an oar and push the boat forward yourself instead of forming a committee to develop a process to make something happen with no errors sometime in the future.

Deliver what you can

Where does an 800-pound gorilla sit? Wherever it wants. At Coca-Cola we did gorilla marketing. We had enough marketing clout and resources to overwhelm our competitors in any pitched battle. We knew it. We organized our forces and we won where we choose to win.

800-pound gorilla getty

Our smaller competitors did guerilla marketing using ambushes, sabotage, raids, hit-and-run tactics, and mobility to fight our larger, less mobile, less agile, traditional organization. They won where they could.

If you're switching from a corporate giant to a smaller more entrepreneurial or family venture, choose your battles carefully. You have to deliver. You have to deliver with less resources, less systems, less clout. Learn to be agile. Learn when to pick up the oar yourself. Just don't hit yourself with it.

Leading Through an Extended Pandemic - Marco's Pizza's Recipe for Success

Tony Libardi Marco's Pizza

The Stockdale Paradox provides a powerful framework for leading through an extended pandemic born out of Stockdale's multi-year prisoner of war experience. The heart of it is *"Unwavering faith that you can and will prevail with the discipline to confront the most brutal facts of the current reality."*

Marco's Pizza's president, Tony Libardi and his team are doing just this, achieving historic record-breaking sales, piloting new innovations, signing 89 new store commitments, and opening their 1,000[th] store through the heart of the pandemic. Their recipe for success includes empathy, values, celebrating wins, inspiration and future focus. Libardi took me through his thinking. The recipe and quotes are his.

Confront the most brutal facts of the current reality

Empathy takes precedence

"Leaders who empathize with their people and put their team first are the ones who succeed." Listening, learning and caring "fosters camaraderie rooted in trust, collaboration and service – all of which become key to successfully navigating through hardship."

Marco's has stepped-up communications with franchisees and field leaders and conducted Townhall sessions to better understand and address the needs of all stores and their employees. By prioritizing empathy and gaining perspective, Marco's leaders are now able to make better decisions more quickly than ever before.

While empathy is always central to exceptional leadership, Leo Flanagan of the Center for Resilience argues that focus, pragmatic optimism and empathy are the three most important contributors to the ability to thrive amidst adversity (along with fact-based decision making, agility, balanced goal-setting, engaging in a higher purpose, self-control, grit, and self-reflection.)

Let Core Values Guide Your Business Decisions

"I truly believe the best leaders use culture to drive unprecedented results. Throughout the pandemic, we relied heavily on our core values and cultural beliefs (People First, Business and Community Health) to guide our decision making."

Marco's early and consistent requirement that all employees wear masks and perform daily health checks directly flowed from those values.

As you sink through the mud of pandemic-related uncertainty, shared values must be the bedrock to inspire accountability and serve as a reality check for coming together to get through the pandemic and prevail.

Find the Good

"Wins – big and small – are cause for celebration. By calling attention to these wins, you are creating an opportunity to inspire your team to achieve even greater success."

While the pandemic posed significant challenges, Marco's remained committed to opening new stores and celebrated their 1000th store milestone not only with the hard-working immigrant entrepreneurs behind that particular store, but with the entire franchise system and its loyal customers.

Stress is cumulative. Enhancing everyone's resilience is an essential leadership responsibility. One way to boost morale and work-ethic is celebrating successes - no matter how big or small.

Unwavering faith that you can and will prevail

Being Inspirational Becomes a Requirement

"It is easy to become discouraged in the face of uncertainty, but as a leader it is your responsibility to rise above the circumstances and direct your team toward a positive vision."

Marco's leadership has succeeded in getting its people to think beyond 'survival mode.' Marco's people have been donating to their communities, hosting birthday party parades for families, innovating with PPE, volunteering to trial virtual kitchens and other innovations.

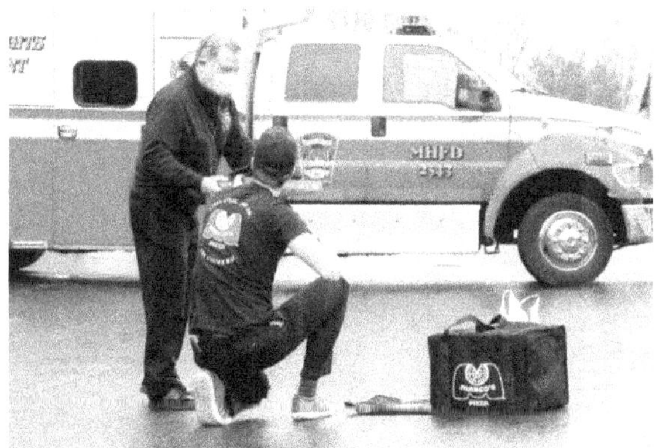

Donating pizza to first responders Marco's Pizza

Inspiration unleashes motivation. A pragmatically optimistic mindset is what team members need from their leaders – especially in the face of uncertainty. Give people something to look forward to and help them understand how the work they do each day makes a difference.

Assemble a Permanent Task Force for the Future

Stockdale talks about "unwavering faith" - not blind faith. Agility is essential. Libardi said "Our leadership team meets daily to discuss trends and adjustments we need to make to stay ahead of changes in consumer behavior and government orders."

They're doing this by exploring a new store model, collaborating with manufacturers for robotic kitchens with co-bots, testing virtual kitchen concepts, third-party delivery, automated contact-free delivery, and curbside service.

The pandemic has forced leaders to innovate. Doing this with a future focused task force communicates the value of preparing for the future, and acting on it sooner together.

Giving Libardi the last word: "Leaders must have the courage to stop doing what used to work and move into unchartered territory. Brands that are able to stay ahead and revolutionize their industry will be the ones to emerge stronger than before."

November 10

Three Essentials in Leading Through Adversity — Especially in a New Role

Leading the way getty

In leading through adversity: 1) Honestly and objectively assess the current situation – the good, the bad, and the ugly. 2) Choose your path forward, focusing on what you can influence and impact and letting go of what you cannot change. 3) Inspire and enable others to commit to actions knowing that they (and their work) matters and with confidence in their own abilities to be part of the solution.

Honestly and objectively assess the current situation

As Stockdale put it, this is about confronting the most brutal facts of the current reality. Be clear on the difference between true facts (not open to interpretation,) perceived facts (influenced by biases,) and assumptions (not necessarily based on facts.) These set up your conclusions, choices and actions.

Dig deep to understand what's going on across customers, collaborators, your own capabilities, competitors, and conditions outside your control especially during times of extreme uncertainty:

physically with people, places and things,

emotionally with great empathy – listening and being curious,

financially.

Choose your path forward

Choices follow conclusions. Distinguish between what you can and cannot change. Then focus on pragmatically optimistic outcomes - the first two components of Leo Flanagan's resiliency model.

"Focus:" putting attention to the matters and people at hand.

"Pragmatic optimism:" a belief that the future will be better and that you will have a role in making it so.

Make choices about what you both can and choose to accomplish and the impact you can and choose to have with what effect.

Inspire and enable others to commit to actions

Leadership is about inspiring and enabling others to do their absolute best together to realize a meaningful and rewarding shared purpose. Build on your situation assessment and choices to inspire and enable others to move towards that better future.

If you tell them what to do, the best you can get is compliance. If you sell, test or consult with them to get their input, they can contribute. Contribution is fine. But, if you want their commitment, they need to co-create the path to that future so they own it. That's an essential first step in helping them believe they matter and build confidence in their own abilities to deliver.

Enabling success has several components:

Clarify what's getting decided and done by whom by when with what resources. This is partly about balanced goal setting – with measurable milestones and goals. It also enables self-control to limit distractions and avoid multi-tasking.

Monitor progress, recognizing, appreciating, and celebrating success and adjusting along the way with the agility to experiment and then quickly change course to achieve interim and overall objectives in the face of challenges. This is partly about self-reflection – objectively reviewing past behaviors, attitudes, perspectives and results.

Keep going with the grit to persevere towards your chosen future.

Taking charge following a sudden promotion

Onboarding into new leadership roles is especially risky during challenging times. While the basics of onboarding and leading through adversity apply, keep three things in mind.

1.   You can't control the situation but you can re-frame what it means. So, prepare in advance as much as possible; be ready to adjust as required. Take a stop – even if only for a few minutes – to assess your predecessor's legacy, the current situation, and choose your path to a brighter future. Secure the resources and support you need. Then, go with the flow, regaining control of the situation as much as you can, and jumping into the dirty work as appropriate.

2.   It's hard to make a clean break. So, take control of your own message and transition as much as you can. Know that everyone is scared and their only question is "What about me?" Meet them where they are on Maslow's hierarchy. Manage the announcement cascade. Secure your base, ensuring your "old" area's ongoing success, and recognizing the people who helped you along the way.

3.   There is no honeymoon, especially during times of adversity. So, set direction and generate momentum quickly after your start, inspiring and enabling the players to commit or recommit to action. In a crisis, think physical safety, reputation and finances – in that order. In any case, evolve the stated and defacto strategies, improve operations, and strengthen your organization as you lead through and out of adversity.

Why Optionality is Key to Post-Pandemic Planning

Optionality getty

In normal times, leaders can choose between three strategic postures: shape, adapt, or reserve the right to play. However, for the vast majority of organizations, the only viable posture coming out of the pandemic is the third, reserving the right to play, keeping their options open. The virus has shown itself resistant to shaping. Those trying to adapt after the pandemic will find themselves trailing the leaders for a very long time.

So, think through the potential scenarios and invest the resources required to reserve your right to play and get out of the starting blocks early once you know which scenario is coming true.

Those successfully shaping a market get to make the market's rules, limiting others' degrees of freedom. Witness Apple, effectively creating the smart phone market and reaping unfair returns for literally decades.

Those choosing a fast-follow or adapting strategic posture choose to let others innovate and then leverage their own strengths to build their business once they know which way the wind is blowing. Coca-Cola, for example, has been a fast-follower in new beverages. They let others pave the way and then either buy them or run a similar beverage through their superior manufacturing and distribution system as soon as those new beverages are ready to scale.

These approaches work when customers, collaborators, capabilities, competitors and conditions are behaving normally so people can make rational predictions of what's going to happen.

That is most definitely not the case now. The only thing you can even come close to controlling is your own capabilities. Fauci expects vaccines to be available by April. But that's just his current best estimate. The virus is controlling conditions. No one really knows how it will mutate and play out. And no one knows how your customers, collaborators and competitors are going to adapt to those changing conditions.

Scenario Planning

Of course, you want to do scenario planning. But all these unknowns will make the scenario planning coming out of the pandemic materially different than what you did going in.

Going into the pandemic, well-run organizations laid out what they thought were the most likely, best, and worst-case scenarios. They then quickly cut and reallocated resources to enable them to survive the worst-case scenario, building back as they could.

If you do the same coming out of the pandemic, you run the risk of getting caught in the middle.

- Those that bet right and re-build the right capabilities in the right place at the right time will shape the market and reap out-sized rewards.
- Those that bet wrong and re-build too many capabilities in the wrong places will suffer material financial losses.
- Those that choose not to ramp up resources until they have more certainty will neither reap "bet right" rewards nor suffer with those that bet wrong. But they won't be able to meet increasing demand and will lose market share – over time.

Keeping your options open

Options have a price. The thesis is that, in this case, you're better off having a call option on resources than you are either ramping them up ahead of time or waiting.

If you are a design/innovation-focused organization, secure your options by keeping your 1st level designers engaged and having those skilled at commercializing those ideas on call. This may involve putting outside developers on low-level retainers so they'll be available when you need them.

If you are production-focused, you need to keep supply-chain, production, and distribution options open. You may literally want to purchase commodity options so you ensure your supply, knowing you can walk away from those options as required. You may want to have a skeleton crew keeping your plants running or have contract manufacturers on retainer.

If you are distribution-focused, you've likely built a web of alliances already. You do need to make sure enough of your allies survive the pandemic for your entire eco-system to continue to function. If you're not sure they are going to survive, you may want to bring in some other redundant allies just-in-case.

If you are service-focused, you can preserve options by ensuring you've got people indoctrinated in your culture and trained on your delivery before they are needed. In this case, you're buying an option by investing in onboarding, socialization and training ahead of the concrete need.

November 18

How PG&E's New CEO Patti Poppe Must Adapt To Break Its Death Spiral

Ultimately, California's largest utility, PG&E, has to be a service-focused company. They can't get there without fixing their ability to deliver without burning down the state. The good news is that their newly appointed CEO, Patti Poppe, has arrows in her quiver in that she's got both delivery and service experience. She's going to have to prioritize fixing delivery first and then turn her attention to service.

This is straight out of Jack Welch's two-step at GE. When he first took over as CEO as "Neutron Jack," he cut all businesses in which the company could not be #1 or #2. Then he cut the bottom performing 10% of the workforce. Then he cut the bottom performing 10% of management. Having re-set that base, he then invested heavily in strengthening GE's people and practices, paving the way for accelerated growth in areas like medical technology, finance, TV and services.

It's a good model for Poppe: 1) Really make safety the top priority, really driving accountability at all levels. 2) Once that is in place, start evolving the culture to be more service-oriented. The first is an exercise in converging and adapting. The second is about evolving.

Converging

If there was ever a leader that needed to take advantage of the time between accepting and starting, it's Poppe. The public announcement came out this morning. Her first official day is January 4, 2021. Per my earlier article on talking advantage of the Fuzzy Front End, Poppe should put together her plan (with the help of interim CEO Smith,) get set up, and invest in relationships and learning. A critical part of that plan is crafting her message.

There's nothing wrong with the way she's being positioned in the announcement of her appointment. It makes all the sense in the world to focus first on providing "safe, reliable, affordable, and clean energy to millions of customers." At one level, no one's going to argue with that.

However, per my earlier article on "What PG&E's Next CEO Must Do To Break Its Death Spiral," Poppe will be leading PG&E out of multiple, compound crises. Almost everyone she'll come into contact with is terrified. PG&E customers are afraid they won't get the energy they need. It's employees all think they're about to get fired. Its board members think they're about to go to jail. The communities in which it operates in are afraid of the next fire. And everyone's afraid of the pandemic.

Poppe need to connect emotionally, rationally and inspirationally, starting with emotionally. That's the #1 task for her Fuzzy Front End. At every moment, with everyone she comes into contact with over the next six months, she has to converge with relationships first.

Of course, that converging will run through her first few weeks as well. If she comes in with the answer and tells people what to do, the best she can ever hope for is compliance. If she wants others to contribute, she has to invite that contribution and value their contributions. If she wants people to commit to a brighter future, she has to let them co-create it.

Evolve

Ideally, Poppe would pivot from converging to evolving within her first few weeks as CEO. That will be the moment she pulls her leadership team together and tells them she's learned enough to co-create the future with them.

The purpose, choices and communication framework from my earlier article on What PS&G's Next CEO Must Do still works:

Purpose: Poppe and her team must align around what they're trying to do over the short and long-term to move beyond just the "transmission and delivery of energy." Poppe's words from her announcement are better, "powering one of the world's largest economies," but still may not go far enough. The purpose needs to inspire.

Choices: Poppe and her team need to make clear choices around how they're going to fix their current problems and how they're going to hold themselves and each other accountable.

Communication: Just as Poppe's going-in communication needs to be emotional, rational and inspirational, her leadership and organization's communication about its purpose and choices need to be the same going forward.

Let's be clear. This organization is in deep trouble. It's employees, customers and communities need Poppe to lead it well.

Why It's Especially Important to See Glasses as Half-Full This Thanksgiving

1/2 Full getty

Everyone on the planet has had issues this year. And we're not yet through the dark times. It's so easy to focus on all the bad things. But the way you feel is hugely influenced by what you pay attention to. That's why it's so important to pay attention to the good things making your glass half-full versus all that's missing. Do this at work and at home – even if those two places are the same – with others and with yourself.

Glass half-empty at work

You know those people. You might even be one of them. Show them anything and they'll tell you what's wrong with it or how to make it better. They think they're helping. For the most part, their intentions are positive as they break things down to build them up better. They may be right. But it still hurts.

And it doesn't have to.

Glass half-full at work

Others lead with the positive. They tell you what works, what you've done well. Then they give you suggestions for how to make it even better. "Even better" feels much better than fixing "what's wrong."

<u>Itemized Response</u>

This is the heart of the itemized response I learned from Roger Neil when he was at Synectics:

1. Ask questions for clarification
2. Point out what's strong and working well
3. Suggest ways to make it even better

Asking questions for clarification demonstrates interest. Pointing out what's strong and working well makes your audience feel appreciated which makes them more open to your suggestions.

<u>Constructive criticism</u>

Leading with the positive can be the difference between destructive and constructive criticism:

1. Itemize merits and concerns
2. Discuss how to retain the merits and eliminate concerns
3. Summarize

The important point here is the balance of working with others to retain the merits of what they are doing or proposing while helping them eliminate concerns.

<u>Building</u>

By definition, building starts with something good. Instead of trying to make that something even better or eliminating any concerns about that something, you're just adding value.

1. Acknowledge connection
2. Add value: modify, add benefits, other applications, new ways to realize original intent
3. Check back with idea owner to make sure you've preserved their idea

Acknowledging the connection to the starting point credits the owner's contribution. Adding value is the heart of the build. The difference between modifying and criticizing is that you're suggesting the modification instead of just pointing out the fault or concern. Checking back with the owner keeps them in charge as idea owner.

Glass half-empty at home

I know this will come as a shock to many of you, but the people in your homes have feelings too. While it's often harder for them to quit than it is for the people you work with, they too can change what they choose to pay attention to. Shame on you if you're not giving them at least as much support and confidence reinforcement as you give to the people you work with. Criticism hurts at home as well as at work.

Glass half-full at home

The same work techniques are applicable at home.

When someone in your home shares an idea or shows you something they're doing, do your own itemized response. Ask questions to demonstrate your interest. Point out what's strong to make them feel appreciated and then more open to your suggestions.

Make your criticism constructive by striking a balance to retain the merits of what they've got while helping them eliminate concerns.

Build on their ideas in a way that helps them retain psychological ownership of their ideas.

Seeing your own glass half-full versus half-empty

There are errors of commission and omission.

Focusing on the errors of omission is a path to despair. The number of great jobs we didn't take, companies we didn't invest in, horses we didn't bet on is almost infinite. They're all in the half-empty part of the glass.

Conversely, even the errors of commission gave you experiences to learn from. Pay attention to the job you did take, the company you did invest in, the people in your life. They're in the half-full part of the glass. Be thankful for all of them. It will make them and you happier this Thanksgiving and beyond.

What Biden Should Do Now to Accelerate Progress in His First 100-Days

McConnell and Biden (and Elaine Chou) CQ-Roll Call, Inc via Getty Images

The election was a split-decision with Biden winning the Presidency, Republicans making gains in the House, and control of the Senate yet to be determined. There's no doubt that the more President Joe Biden can reach across the aisle, the more effective his Presidency will be. He should start doing that now by involving the other side in his early appointments and executive orders.

Persuasion framework

Bryan Smith lays out a useful framework of persuasion in "The Fifth Discipline Field Book." He suggests five approaches:

Co-create – Consult – Test – Sell - Tell

Tell is what the traffic cop on the corner does. They tell. You comply.

Sell is used by someone trying to persuade someone else that their idea is right, as is.

Test is used by someone looking for a read on the viability of an idea before selling it.

Consult is about getting others to help improve an idea.

Co-create happens when people start with a blank page and build the idea together.

Where we are

Currently, those in power tell others what to do and they do it. Witness the number of votes in the House and Senate that split on party lines. Witness the number of Presidential executive orders.

Those getting told what to do comply if they must, while actively looking for ways to get around or undercut the things they disagree with. They spend their free time thinking about what they're going to do to get back at their oppressors when they get the chance.

More of the same will likely produce more of the same.

Reaching across the aisle

"The refusal of Democrats and Republicans to cooperate with one another is not some mysterious force beyond our control. It's a decision, a choice we make. And if we can decide not to cooperate, then we can decide *to* cooperate." – Joe Biden, November 7

Biden and Senate Majority Leader Mitch McConnell were both in the Senate when the moderates from either party swung votes. That was a time when cooperation was more productive than confrontation. And Biden was VP when McConnell set denying Obama (and Biden) a second term as his top legislative priority and then refused to consent to any new Supreme Court Justices in Obama's last year in office.

If anyone's going to reach across the aisle, Biden is going to have to make the first move. The rest of his early appointments and upcoming early executive orders give him his first, best opportunities to do that

The current most likely scenario is that the Senate will challenge and then advise and consent to most of Biden's cabinet appointments. Executive orders don't need Senate concurrence which is why people from the Obama administration are advising Biden to use them liberally. But that's telling.

Instead, Biden can reach across the aisle by inviting Republicans to consult on or co-create these early decisions. This means at least asking for their ideas and input so they can contribute to the conversation and have some influence on the choices. The more Republican suggestions that are incorporated, up to and including putting Republican in the Cabinet, the more Republicans will feel valued, part of the consensus, and closer to committing to moving forward together.

Fuzzy Front End

In executive onboarding, the Fuzzy Front End is the time between accepting and starting a job. A couple of the most important things to do in this period are jump-starting relationships and crafting your new leader's 100-day action plan. Jump-starting relationships can be about making emotional connections with people you're meeting for the first time, or it can be about sorting out your go-forward leadership team in a merger or acquisition.

This is, of course, exactly what we're talking about here for Biden.

He's meeting McConnell and all the other members of congress for the first time as President-elect. As newly crowned Henry V said to Falstaff, "Presume not that I am the thing I was." Biden gets to re-set their relationships so all hopefully decide to cooperate – or are at least open to the possibility.

He's sorting out his go-forward leadership team, teeing up Cabinet and other appointments – hopefully with Republican input and participation.

And, following on from FDR, Biden and his team are mapping out their 100-day action plan – hopefully inviting the Republicans in to cooperate.

December 8

How to Keep Your Communication Plans from Getting Derailed by Leaks

Telling secrets AFP/Getty Images

Not going to happen. If you think leaks are not going to happen, you're wrong. With the Internet, everyone is a publisher. So, everyone can leak your plans. You have to assume leaks are going to happen. And, if you think you can keep them from derailing your carefully laid out communication plans, you're wrong again. That's not going to happen either. You're only viable option is to assume there's going to be a leak somewhere along the way, do what you can to control your communication as long as possible, and have second phase ready for when you lose control.

The problem

People want to be in the room where it happens. If they're not, they dig around until they find a way in or find out what's going on. If they are in the room where it happens, they want others to know how important they are. These collide into a bias for leaks.

Furthermore, the Internet is a conduit. It breaks down the walls between internal and external communication. Internal memos get forwarded externally. Internal talks get videoed and shared externally. And everyone has access to outside information all the time.

The framework

So, things are going to leak. The issue is that disrupts your ability to control your communication. For major announcements, follow these steps:

1) Set the action plan. This is the substance of what you're going to announce. Messaging should flow from your actual plan, not the other way around.
2) Set the first phase of the communication plan. This includes your message and who hears what, when and from whom. Know that everyone's main question is "What does this mean for me?" In general, you want to tell:
    i. Those emotionally impacted first. They should hear one-on-one in a place that allows them to express their emotions.
    ii. Those directly impacted second. They should hear in small groups in a setting that allows them to ask questions to better understand the changes.
    iii. Those indirectly or not impacted last. They can hear through mass communication.
3) Have a second phase ready to activate when the first phase of your communication leaks. Know that every additional person you read into the change decreases the likely time to the first leak. It's not that they will leak intentionally. It's that their knowing and changing something they normally do adds one more datapoint to someone else's picture.

Your second phase of your communication plan will probably look like a crisis management plan:

    i.   Prepare in advance. The better you have anticipated possible scenarios, the more prepared you will be, and the more confidence you'll have when leaks occur. (Which they will.)

    ii.   React to events. The reason you prepared is so that you can react quickly and flexibly to the situation you face. Don't over-think this. Do what you prepared to do.

    iii.   Bridge the gaps. The big gap is going to be in the order in which people hear about the changes.

- If the leak happens before you've told those emotionally impacted, divide and conquer and get to them as soon as practical. In the absence of a leak, you could have told them sequentially. Now you'll have to get to them in parallel. Then go on to the directly impacted and finally those indirectly impacted.

- If the leak happens after you've told those emotionally impacted, but before you get to those directly impacted, gather them up as soon as practical and tell them. Then go on to those indirectly impacted.

- If the leak happens just before you've told those indirectly impacted, there's less to worry about. Still, you should accelerate your mass message if you can.

Some practical thoughts

The shorter the time between when you tell the first person and your mass communication, the less likely things will leak during your communications.

Know you're going to miss one or more emotionally impacted people. This is generally because you did not anticipate them being emotionally impacted. When that happens, take the hit. Apologize. Tell them what you know. Let them vent. And move one.

How to Beat the Odds and Make Equal Partnerships Work

The Wright Brothers getty

Most of the time, equal partnerships are hard to make work because they are not actually equal. Furthermore, even if they are equal for one brief shining moment, they don't stay equal. If you want to beat the odds and make your partnership work, you either need to have a shared interest, a shared framework for making decisions, or the leverage required to influence your partners to do the right things the right way (your way.)

"Partnership: A relationship usually involving close cooperation between parties having specified and joint rights and responsibilities." – Merriam Webster's 3rd definition

Arguably the most critical "specified" rights are decision rights – who makes what decisions. In unequal partnerships in which it's clear who's making which decisions, decision-making generally works. Conversely, equal partners, trying to make all decisions jointly, are generally doomed to failure. Eventually they disagree, get frustrated, and grow apart. The answer to how to make it work is right there in the definition: be specifically and explicitly clear who's making which decisions and how.

Many of my books have been co-authored. Things worked well when one person was the lead author and made the final decisions. Alternately, things worked well when we gave different authors specific responsibilities for specific sections so they could focus on those sections, become experts, and make decisions for "their" sections.

Conversely, it was more challenging when decisions were shared and we had to come to consensus. It's hard to get everyone to agree - especially without an agreed framework for decision making. True for books, businesses, and almost any situation where two or more people have to cooperate with each other. Which gets us right back to shared interest, frameworks and leverage.

Shared Interest

First prize is for partners to share the same context, objectives, and values. Having those in place makes it much easier for you to cooperate and share rights and responsibilities. And having those in place provides a platform for constructive conflict. If your interests are truly shared, you can't help but looking out for each other's best interests at all times. You all can assume positive intent and view differences as arising from complementary strengths.

Trouble arises when situational changes effect different partners differently. These can be changes in their personal situation like marriage, children, or changes in other businesses or occupations. These can be changes in the business situation across customers, collaborators, associates, competitors, or external conditions. Any of these have the ability to change the relative importance of the partnership to the different partners.

Shared Frameworks

As noted in an earlier article, frameworks are the basic conceptual structures that people use to flesh out their ideas. They help people know where to start, and they focus and guide thinking about how to achieve purpose. If you and your partners agree on frameworks for decision-making, it makes it easier for you and everyone you are working with to make decisions. All know what information to look at, what precedents apply and how different people will approach decisions.

Leverage

Leverage is about altering the balance of consequences – often by making unseen consequences visible. The essence of a balance of consequence is the comparison of positive and negative repercussions of making different choices.

Even if your partner can make a decision without you, and even if your partner follows a different decision-making framework, you can still influence that decision by applying leverage.

Remember the marshmallow test? A child is given a marshmallow or pretzel and told they can eat it if they want, but if they wait fifteen minutes, they can have two. The incremental treat is leverage.

Your leverage with your partners is going to range from positive to negative, from small to large, from indirect to direct, and from immediate to deferred. In general, make sure you are:

- Applying positive leverage to reinforce desired choices and actions versus undesired,
- Applying small leverage in doses over time or large leverage when needed urgently,
- Helping others understand the impact of your indirect leverage.
- Helping others understand the short-term versus long-term tradeoffs inherent in your deferred leverage.

Not all partnerships work. Even when they do work, they may not work forever. As you find yourself moving from shared interest to shared frameworks to leverage, be on the lookout for the moment when it's time to stop partnering at all.

How to Gain Leadership Experience Without Experience

Marin Alsop leading the Vienna Orchestra AFP via Getty Images

While artistic and scientific leaders can build strengths on their own for the most part, interpersonal leaders' essential ability to interconnect can be built only by doing it. Strengths are made up of innate talents, learned knowledge, and practice-honed skills. Those are mostly individual gifts or activities while interpersonal leadership is … wait for it … interpersonal - which can be developed only by actually leading others. Square the circle by ratcheting up your experience with a current best leadership approach.

If leadership is about inspiring and enabling others to do their absolute best together to realize a meaningful and rewarding shared purpose (which it is,) then you can't lead without interconnecting with the "others." The challenge, especially as an executive onboarding into a new leadership role, is how to gain that experience without having that experience.

Build on innate talent with learning, practice and experience.

By the time musicians get to their first rehearsal with others in an ensemble, they will have learned the music and practiced their particular parts to a level of unconscious competence. Their rehearsals are not about learning or practicing their individual parts more, but about gaining experience interconnecting all the different parts of the ensemble into a complete, finished piece of music.

How then do you gain experience with a complete, finished leadership approach? How do you get the job if you haven't done the job? It's easier than you might think. Take a current best leadership approach in your current role or in roles in project, program, temporary, interim, or pilot leadership.

Current Best Leadership Approach

Just as the current best thinking approach ratchets up thinking, the current best leadership approach ratchets up leadership. The former requires the thinker to be vulnerable and put their current best thinking on the table for all to improve together. The latter requires the leader to be vulnerable and do the same with their current best leadership approach.

It actually makes more sense since you can think on your own, but you can't lead on your own. Of course, this only works if you are one of the 20% of leaders with enough self-confidence to be open to learning from and with others.

Understand this likely requires two mindset shifts. You must:

1. Be self-confident enough to be vulnerably open to help in ratcheting up your own current best leadership approach.
2. Not let titles and formal job descriptions get in the way of your proactively ratcheting up your leadership experience.

Current Role

Gain experience for your next role in your current role by thinking and acting like a next-level leader, stepping up from time to time to recommend instead of ask, or even inform instead of recommend.

Project and Program

Functional leaders often get their general management chops in project or program leadership roles. These provide great opportunities to gain the experience of leading others with different expertise.

Temporary or Interim

If you're in a temporary or interim role, understand whether you're there "holding the fort until we find the right person, which absolutely will not be you," "on probation with a good chance of becoming permanent," or "doing the job as a developmental opportunity on the way to something else." In any case, treat it like the chance to experience interconnecting that it is.

Pilot

Pilot roles are developmental by nature. Jump at chances to get experience leading smaller, simpler teams, units, geographies, or businesses before moving on to run larger, more complicated ones.

How to ratchet up leadership

Prepare in advance. Make sure you're ready to lead. Learn everything you can. Practice leadership skills. Create your 100-Day Personal Action Plan. Get set up. Jump-start relationships.

Experience the experience. Whether it's your current role, a project, program, or temporary, interim, or pilot assignment, it is real. In a sense, there is no dress rehearsal for real life. In another sense, every day gives you the opportunity to learn from your experiences together and do better the next day. Do your best. Adjust to what goes wrong. Be open to help from others. And move on.

Say thank you. When you're done, and ready to move on to the next step, thank everyone for their help.

December 29

Applying the Current Best Thinking Framework to Your Own Career Development

Robert Joss Fairfax Media via Getty Images

If you are the best you can be, the only way to go is down. Couple that with former Stanford Business School dean, Robert Joss's insight that only 20% of leaders have the confidence required to be open to help and the only possible conclusion is that we're all works in progress and we should all invest in improving ourselves – with others' help. Accept that you're in charge of you. Get help. Build on your Current Best Thinking to bridge the gap between your current reality and future possibilities.

Roger Neill designed his Current Best Thinking framework for problem solving. It's easily applied to your own career development if you have the confidence accept that there is a problem to solve and that others can help you solve it. What follows is an adaptation of Roger's framework to apply to your own career development at any stage of your career. First, core premises:

1) You're in charge of you. Own your own career development. Certainly, get help from others. But no victims allowed. No blaming circumstances or anyone else. You are both the problem and the problem owner.

2) Get help. You know the value of getting diverse perspectives on problem solving. Invite and cherish those diverse perspectives on your own career development. Treat others input as gifts.

3) Build on your Current Best Thinking. This is a combination of career planning 101 and gap-bridging problem-solving. Start with future possibilities, objectives and goals. Step back and assess the current reality. Then deploy the Current Best Thinking problem-solving approach to generate ideas. Turn those into a remedy. Commit to specific actions.

1. **Future Possibilities**. Start with possibilities. What would make you happier? Recall, happiness is three goods. What's the right blend for you going forward of i) doing good for others, ii) doing things you're good at, and iii) doing good for yourself? What do you really want in terms of relationships, health and well-being, financial rewards and your own emotional state? Pull those together into long-term career objectives and short-term goals

2. **Current Reality.** Get help doing a brutally honest assessment of where you are now. How much impact are you really having on others? What are your current strengths and gaps? What's the real balance of your current relational, physical, financial and emotional bank accounts?

3. **Current Best Thinking.** Think through potential options to bridge these gaps.

Pull it all together into your current best thinking around a) your picture of success, b) your current reality, and c) how to bridge the gaps.

Share that going-in perspective with those that have agreed to help you. Where Roger's approach generally works better in a group so people can build off each other's ideas, you'll most likely want to do this one-on-one so no one holds back for fear of embarrassing you in front of others.

Answer their questions for clarification to help them understand context and your best current thinking, not for them to comment on or improve the thinking – yet.

Ask them to highlight the most positive of your best current thinking – so you start by feeling good.

Ask them to identify the key barriers keeping your best current thinking from working. Get all the barriers on the table at the same time before working any of them.

Decide on the most important barrier to work.

4.   **Ideas => Remedy**. Bat ideas on how to fix most important barrier back and forth: WYDIS (What You Do Is.) How you react to their ideas is critical. If you're at all defensive, they'll hold back.

Pull the ideas together into a possible remedy to that barrier (testing.)

If the possible remedy is not strong enough, continue to work this barrier. If the remedy works, determine whether that is enough to solve the overall problem and move your forward towards your objectives and goals. If yes, move on to action steps. If not, work the next most important barrier.

5.   **Action Steps:** Commit to what you're going to do by when to make this theoretical solution real changing yourself from problem owner to solution owner.

About the author

George Bradt has led the revolution in how people start new jobs - accelerating transitions so leaders and their teams reduce their rates of failure and fulfill potential. After Harvard and Wharton (MBA), he progressed through sales, marketing, and general management roles around the world at Unilever, Procter & Gamble, Coca-Cola, and J.D. Power's Power Information Network spin off as chief executive. Now he is Chairman of PrimeGenesis executive onboarding, author of 9+ books on onboarding and leadership, over 650 columns for Forbes, and 17 musical plays, plays and screenplays (book, lyrics & music).

Onboarding & leadership books authored or co-authored by George Bradt:

- The New Leader's 100-Day Action Plan (John Wiley & Sons, 4th edition 2016)
- Onboarding: How to Get Your New Employees up to Speed in Half the Time (John Wiley & Sons, 2009)
- The Total Onboarding Program: An Integrated Approach (Wiley/Pfeiffer, 2010)
- First-Time Leader (John Wiley & Sons, 2014)
- The New Job 100-Day Plan (GHP Press, 2012)
- Point of Inflection (GHP Press 2017-19)
- CEO Boot Camp (GHP Press 2019)
- The New Leader's Playbook (GHP Press – each year 2011-2020)
- Executive Onboarding Volumes I - IV (GHP Press 2020)
- Influence and Impact (John Wiley & Sons, 2021)

George can be reached at gbradt@primegenesis.com

Created especially for
you.....

Everyone needs
'A Little Black Book'.
A place to write 'secret
things' and to write 'stuff'
that you think about and
want to remember - and
not want to remember.
'A Little Black Book' is that
prized and treasured
notebook
that you keep close to your
heart.
The 'Little Black Book' that
takes you on journeys of
memories - and prepares
you for the next one.
Everything you need will be
in here.